gs from

May

o' Sand"

The Insider's Guide to
CAPE MAY

AN **EXIT ZERO** PUBLICATION

The Insider's Guide to CAPE MAY

AN  EXIT ZERO PUBLICATION

By JACK WRIGHT,
STEFANIE GODFREY
& Friends

Edited & designed by Jack Wright

© 2004 by Beach Plum Press

Beach Plum Press

ISBN 0-9729296-1-4

CONTENTS

About this Book
This is the bit that tells you why we published it and why you should read it

I'M guessing you've picked up this delightful little book for one of the following reasons:

1. You're new, or fairly new, to Cape May and you're thinking, "Gee whizz, this looks neat. My all-in-one guide to the coolest things to do in this great little resort town. I should buy this." (You're right – you should.)

2. You're a Cape May veteran but even you know there might be some things you've missed and, besides, you think *Exit Zero* is an all-over smashing periodical and you're thinking, "If those guys at *Exit Zero* did this, then this book is probably informative, inspiring and entertaining. I should buy this." (You're right – you should.)

3. Your family came over on the Mayflower, you've lived here all your life, dozens of your ancestors are buried at Cold Spring, you know this town inside out and you're thinking, "The Insider's Guide? Who are these jokers kidding! There isn't one single thing in here that's news to me, but I'll take a look any-

Another glorious sunset down at the Cove. *Photo: Craig Terry*

way." (You're wrong – we hope. Buy it anyway, for a friend.)

4. You're really, really bored. It's probably raining and your girlfriend/boyfriend/wife/husband/sugarmomma is poring over a book about the Atkins Diet/lighthouses/embroidery/classic cars/liposuction, you've got nothing better to do, and you're thinking, "Is this relationship really working?" (Not our problem, talk to a relationship counselor – and buy the book already.)

Inside these pages you'll discover some cool things that you would never, ever, ever have known about otherwise. These are the things that a **No. 2** or a **No. 3** from the above list would know about. There's nothing illegal or anything (apart from the human sacrifices that happen on Higbees Beach every Saturday at 3am between Labor Day and Columbus Day – see page 123), just stuff that's off the beaten path (often literally). We should add that there is also a lot of what you might regard as obvious, but we present it in a refreshing and enthusiastic way. We love this town, and we want to spread that love around as much as possible (though we practice safe love and hope that you do, too).

Finally, if you're wondering how this exquisitely-produced book only costs $10 when there are slim little paperbacks in black and white on the bookshelves for that same price, this is because we were supported by the advertisers in the listings section. I'd like to thank them for their support and hope you will spend lots of your money on them – they are, after all, the creme de la creme in this town. I hope you enjoy the book.

Jack Wright Editor/Publisher, *Exit Zero*

World War Two lookout tower at Sunset Beach. *Photo: Zoey Sless-Kitain*

About this Town
A random list of things that might or might not be useful and/or interesting

YOU'RE on vacation — we realize that. You don't want a geography or a history lesson — we realize that, too. But if you're a new or newish visitor, a local or a long-term visitor who doesn't pay attention, there are some useful, if not enlightening, things you should know about Cape May. Here are the 26 most interesting ones.

1. Cape May is an island, hence the name Cape Island, which you'll sometimes see bandied around town on signs and things. Don't feel foolish if you never knew this. It never used to be an island — it only became one when a canal was built in 1943 to provide a protective shipping lane during the Second World War.

2. Within this four-square-mile island are four, yes four, separate municipalities — Cape May (pop. 4,034), Cape May Point (pop. 241), West Cape May (pop. 1,095) and Lower Township (23,978, though only a small portion of Lower is on the island). Each of these has its own mayor and council – and until 2001 they had separate police forces, too. You might think this rather

A clam boat at Cape May's bustling harbor. *Photo: Stephen Spagnuola*

unnecessary. You would not be alone, with all due respect to the hard-working mayors, council members and commissioners.

4. If you study our map on Pages 16-17, which denotes the boundaries in red, you'll see that during the course of a five-minute walk from a certain point on Sunset Boulevard to West Perry Street you can pass through all four municipalities.

5. Cape May becomes West Cape May at around Swain's hardware store — sometimes you'll see officers from the Cape May Border Patrol around there, carrying out random searches.

6. West Cape May is a dry town.

7. Cape May Point has a centuries-long vampire problem and is a very easy place in which to get lost. But still, go there and get lost because it has a fascinating, utterly random collection of houses and styles.

8. Just kidding (about the vampire bit).

9. There's another town, North Cape May, which begins over the other side of the West Cape May Bridge. And here's a secret we probably shouldn't be sharing — North Cape May has a beautiful, secluded beach that is only used by locals (who are usually too busy making money from the likes of you to have time for sunbathing).

10. Cape May became the first known seaside resort in America when people from Philly started arriving by steamboat around 1801, which was also the last time the Eagles won an NFC playoff game.

11. At one time, Cape May rivaled Newport, Rhode Island,

It's only Page 11, and we're on our third sunset picture already. Concrete Ship with the ferry in the background. *Photo: Stephen Spagnuola*

as the toniest seaside resort in the country. Four presidents vacationed here (all of them staying at Congress Hall), as did leading dignitaries and gentlemen from both North and South. The Civil War and a huge fire in 1878, which wiped out 35 acres of hotels and beachfront real estate, changed all that.

12. The slogan "Cool Cape May" was coined by the city council in 1896. We at *Exit Zero* have readopted that phrase and champion it at every opportunity. Back then, the phrase referred to the pleasing affect achieved by the breezes coming in from both the Atlantic and the Delaware Bay as opposed to the meaning adopted by jazz musicians in the 1930s.

13. It's impossible for a gentleman to buy a pair of pants, a nice shirt or a dress jacket in Cape May. Shorts, sure. Flip-flops, baseball caps, T-shirts, no problem. So if anyone out there has a few bucks rolling around in their bank account and they like the idea of opening up a cool little men's boutique, then would you please come do it? It would probably do rather well.

14. Women do not have this problem — there are several excellent women's stores in Cape May.

15. When you get here, find a good place to park your car, and if the sun is shining, leave it there until you're ready to go home. Then rent some bikes for your whole stay. Cape May is a wonderful place to ride, whether you're going for a ramble or going to dinner.

16. Always, always lock your bike. This is a pleasant and safe town and no one steals bikes for monetary gain or because they're a bad person; they take them because they're too drunk to drive home from the bars. If you were to drive around, you'd likely find your bike lying in someone's garden.

17. Obey those 25mph speed limits, especially on Lafayette and Washington Streets — those pesky police cars are hiding in side streets and they WILL ticket you at 35mph.

18. Who'd want to speed through this gorgeous town anyway?

19. Be aware that locals hate Surrey bikes, so try and be a wee bit thoughtful and maybe pull over to the side if you're slowing down the traffic. Better still, don't rent one — any idea of how silly you look in one?

20. Don't restrict your visits to the summer time. One

Far from the Victoriana of the Historic District, the harbor has constant reminders of Cape May's status as a fishing port. *Photo: Stephen Spagnuola*

of the best-kept secrets around here is October/November. Some grumpy locals consider it their favorite month — this is because all the tourists have gone, it's sometimes still in the 70s and the sunsets bathe the whole town in an orange glow, because by this time of year the sun is no longer hiding around the corner (geographically speaking), where the lighthouse is.

21. If you're from Manhattan or Morristown, NJ, be aware that you're on Cape May time, or, as the locals would say, you're in Cape Maybe. Things don't run like clockwork here. You can tell by the way people talk. This town is below the Mason-Dixon line — you're in the South, folks, so lighten your load and settle into the local way of things and you'll be much happier. Isn't

this one of the reasons you came here — to get languid? People from Philly have been coming here for centuries, so they already know this. Plus, everyone knows Philly types are also a bit on the slow side.

22. Most important of all, when you're here, make sure you never miss Cape May's bible of entertainment, *Exit Zero*. That's the funny, fascinating, useful, zesty, feisty periodical that publishes every Thursday in the summer months and also comes out periodically in the spring, winter and fall. You'll see it in stores, restaurants, bars, B&Bs and hotels and motels all over town. You can keep in touch when you're back home by subscribing. Email us — subscribe@exitzero.us — and we'll send you the details.

23. You WILL be given a ticket if you go on the beach after dark (trust us, we know), especially if you go skinny-dipping. In fact, for some reason, the cops always seem to show up when limber young ladies go skinny-dipping. So if you're going to do it, budget in an extra $65 a head for your stay here.

24. If you're going to skinny-dip, don't do it right in front of Carney's and Cabanas, at Beach between Jackson and Decatur (trust us, we know).

25. Jackson Street is the 13th most haunted street in America. We must admit that our sources for this are really sketchy.

26. Cape May has the best sunsets on the east coast of America. Our evidence for this is, much like No. 25, largely anecdotal. But come here on a clear, sunny day in summer, fall or winter and tell us we're wrong.

Sunset Beach in February. *Photo: Zoey Sless-Kitain*

CHAPTER ONE
The Great Outdoors

Around the Beaches

Whether you want to people watch, birdwatch, or ferry watch, there's a patch of sand waiting for you...

WILD guess, but the main reason you're here is Cape May's most valuable natural asset – its beautiful beaches. Unless you know this town pretty well, there are more options than you might be aware of.

Cape May You've all seen this one. Chances are you're sitting on it right now reading this book. It's a pretty impressive big strand of beach, but it used to be a great deal larger. In the 19th century, the town was nationally-famous for the huge expanse of fine, white sand. But after decades of erosion, a beach replenishment program was begun in the 1980s, employing more than one million engineers who waded into the ocean, scooped up little buckets of sand then walked back to the beach and deposited the sand back where it belonged. Kinda like that classic war movie, *The Great Escape*, where the prisoners would dig a tunnel and hide the dirt in their pockets. Okay, so maybe that's not what happened, but the end result is that Cape May once again has a fine and splendid beach. Not as big

Madison Chamberlain at the bay beach. *Photo: Maciej Nabrdalik*

Ben Isenhart and Bela Lotozo at the Cove. *Photo: Maciej Nabrdalik*

as Wildwood's, six miles up the coast, but do you really need to hail a cab to take you from your deck chair to the waves? For the beach (which includes Poverty and the Cove), you'll need a tag from Memorial Day to Labor Day. Daily cost is $4, $11 for a week and a bargain $17 if you're lucky enough to need one for the summer. Sand wheelchairs are available, free of charge. Call 884-9520 for more information – it's first-come, first-served.

Fashion/lifestyle tip: Even if you're only around for a day or two, splurge on a beach tag for the whole season and continue to do so year after year, saving the cute little tags as you go. And once you've got a decent collection, pin them to an old faded and worn baseball cap (if you don't own one, buy a pre-faded one from Abercrombie & Fitch). Under no circumstances should you wear this cap with less than five years worth of tags on there – you might as well wear a bright yellow T-shirt with large red letters saying **SHOEBIE**. If you can't wait five years, go on eBay and buy yourself some instant credibility. Think we're kidding? At 9:03pm on Tuesday, March 16, there was a pack of three Cape May tags – 1987, 88 and 96 – on sale for $29.99.

The Cove A big favorite among locals. There's something about the vibe here that is very special. The piping plovers love it, too, and you should be aware that they have first dibs on account of them being a protected species. So don't be elbowing them out of the way – the Rangers will be very, very mad at you and they WILL make you move. The Cove is where most of the surfing goes on. Coming here at 8 o'clock on a sunny summer morning is a pleasure. A whole mixture of folks, from teenagers to fiftysomethings, ride the waves before their day's work begins. If you're not at one with the ocean, lie back with a coffee and a newspaper and watch people spending one minute of their hour at the beach riding their boards, and the other 59 minutes trying to scrabble back on to them.

Poverty Beach A real misnomer this one. Poverty Beach sits at the eastern end of Beach Avenue, facing an ever-growing collection of McMansions, many of which lie empty off-season, which can lend a depressingly lifeless feel to this side of town. In the summer, however, Poverty Beach is a pleasure and it's never as busy as the main beach. You see, this is the constant dilemma we face when writing this book – do we tell you about these things and risk losing the very essence of the place? I guess we just did.

Cape May Point The beaches here are small, intimate and wildly romantic. The Point is a strange and wonderful little town, and the beaches reflect this. These are beaches to go to when you really want some peace to read or think. (They are, though, busier than they used to be on account of the fact that the Point is disappearing into the ocean at an alarming rate. Witness the Concrete Bunker, which sits at the waters edge but which was originally 900 feet from the ocean.) An especially great place for genuflection is the beach on Lake Avenue, where St. Peter's Episcopal Church, a tiny and gorgeous little joint of worship, hugs the corner. At this beach, two wooden chairs provide the perfect spot from which to ponder a moonlight night or a splendid sunrise or sunset.

The other beaches are found at the end of Stites Avenue and at Alexander, which adjoins Sunset Beach and is a top spot for picking Cape May Diamonds. When you're at the Point, make a, um, point of visiting the general store. It's a great little throwback of a place, where you can get a deli sandwich and browse through jars of penny candies and beach toys. By the way, a Cape May beach tag won't wash here – you need to buy one from the Borough of Cape May Point. The better news is that there are no parking meters anywhere in Cape May Point.

Bay Beach Almost exclusively a locals' beach, since most tourists won't be bothered driving over the West Cape May bridge to get here. The Bay Beach has no tags, no lifeguards and not a whole lot of sand either, but it has a quiet, semi-deserted feel that a lot of people like. It's also cool to see the Cape May-Lewes ferry looming large as it heads into dock. Spending a day here and then going for cocktails at nearby Harpoon Henry's (formerly Whaler's Cove) is a must.

The charming little St. Peter's church at Cape May Point. *Photo: Jack Wright*

Higbees Beach A magical spot with a dirty little past. Up until the 90s, people came here, took off their clothes and did unspeakable things, hence Order 3-2-6 introduced by Lower Township which prevents anyone from taking their clothes off and cavorting around on the sand. Offenders face a $1,000 fine and/or 90 days in prison. Thanks to this, Higbees is now a safe place to take your children, though, sadly, some unspeakable things still happen, such as the dropping of beer cans and food wrappers. Isn't it amazing how stupid and thoughtless some idiots can be? If you've ever been to Big Sur, you might see similarities to Higbees, with artistically-twisted pieces of driftwood scattering the narrow, secluded beach. To get here, take New England west until it runs into the little parking lot at Higbees. (We didn't put New England on our map – you'll have to find it yourself.)

Into the West

Susan Tischler recommends two beautiful bike trips
you simply have to take

A SUMMER Sunday morning at the seashore (try saying that
three times real fast) is absolutely one of the best times to go
for a bike ride, at least in Cape May. I don't really know what it's
like to take a summer Sunday morning bike ride at the seashore
anywhere else but I do know what it's like here. Not long ago
I dragged the old, rusty Schwinn out of the garage and went
down to my favorite jumping off point – the pavilion at Beach
Avenue and Broadway. Naturally, the earlier you get started the
better. I don't know about you, but I'm a very nervous biker and
the early bird is least likely to have trouble with traffic, roller
bladers, joggers, and the extra-hazardous and ever-present
boogie-board-on-a-bike person.

So, off I go down Broadway, past the Whimsical Mermaid
gift shop/art gallery, with appropriately enough a mermaid
hanging off the sign. At the light, I turn left on to Sunset where
I encounter many fellow bikers, joggers and power walkers
– in fact, whole families of them. Apparently one can't get up
early enough for these folks. One thing readers should note
and hopefully be encouraged by – I am not (as you may have

Scottie Duffy and Sean Conners (who, unlike the author, are experienced bikers) head down two-mile-long Sunset Boulevard. *Photo: Stephen Spagnuola*

already guessed) the most graceful thing on a bike. I am not confident. I am not skilful. I am in total admiration of people who can mount and dismount on the same side of the bike while it's still in motion. That is so cool. I am, in short, a shaky, twitchy bicyclist. This stems from not having learned to ride a bike until I moved to Cape May at 29 years of age. The truth is, you simply can't live in Cape May and not bike. It's not practical, especially in July and August. So, learn I did. I crashed into Lifeguard boats innocently lying about on the promenade. I crashed into bushes, telephone poles, parked cars. If I saw anyone – I mean anyone – coming toward me either on foot or on a bike, my bicycle would start to teeter and I would crash into something. You don't even want to know how I came to a stop

without crashing into something. Okay, I'll tell you. I'd forget how to brake, you see, and just flay my legs out until they found the pavement with the bicycle still between my legs. Still, I got back up and tried again because biking in Cape May is lovely but also essential for getting from one point to another.

Okay, so now back to the adventure. Because of all of the above reasons, I turn left on to Seagrove Road, instead of continuing on Sunset. This is a lovely country road which the general tourist doesn't know about and a safe haven from traffic and the like. At the end of Seagrove, I turn left on to Lighthouse Ave., heading toward, you guessed it, the lighthouse at Cape May Point State Park. At this stage, you should park and lock your bike and take a tour of the lighthouse or go over to the hawk platform and take a look at the birdies or try one of the nature trails. I don't have that much time this day, besides which, I'm hungry. So, I go back out Lighthouse Ave. – you'll catch a glimpse of Lake Lily on your left – and at the end of the road I turn left on to Sunset again. This time there's no stopping me. I put it into full gear (I have no gears, I just pedal a little harder) and head straight for the Concrete Ship at the end of Sunset. In case you haven't guessed, it's called Sunset because that's the best place to catch the sunset every night. I totter off the bike and walk up to the Sunset Beach Grill and order an egg sandwich with cheese, onion and tomato for $3, a cup of coffee and a bottle of water.

This is what I've been waiting for – a chance to sit on the

Route 607, aka Bayshore Road, will lead you to some enchanting rural landscapes in West Cape May. *Photo: Maciej Nabrdalik*

Get off your bike and climb the 199 steps of the lighthouse. *Photo: Craig Terry*

deck which wraps around the Beach Grill and look out at the ocean, watch the ferry coming in, the fishermen on the beach and "say to myself, what a wonderful world."

The return trip is uneventful and by the time I'm back at the Beach Avenue pavilion, I have biked 6.9 miles and I think to myself "what a good girl am I." So don't be a beach potato, get out, rent a bike and get the arteries flowin'.

Trip No. 2

The Sunset Beach/Cape May Point tour is the usual one visitors take but I'm heading out to Higbees Beach by way of Beach Avenue and Sunset Boulevard. I go along Beach Avenue, heading west, until I come to Broadway – a right turn takes me into West Cape May and I make a left on to Sunset. Look for Highway 607 on your right, about a mile up the road. This is also known as Bayshore Road. Follow it to the end but please stop and look around. You'll pass Rea's Farm which has a great little produce stand at Bayshore and Stevens. If you have a basket on your bike, you can pick up some fresh produce on the way back.

Part of the farmland has been preserved for conservation and you'll note the bird observatory sign on the left, past the farm equipment. If you time it right, you could join up with a group of birders – but there's plenty to see and observe on your own. Roosters crowing in the distance, horses grazing, open land. I think the sweetest sight of my journey was that of an older woman in a flowing skirt biking toward me with a basket of flowers. I don't want a posed picture, nor do I want to intrude upon her, so I leave my camera in the basket, but still she stays in my thoughts. At the end of Bayshore make a left turn on to New England. This is another lovely country road with farms, yucky new construction, a haunted-looking house, an alpaca farm, and a sense of serenity which will lead you to Higbees Beach. The history of Higbees is varied and best explained by the posted sign in the small parking lot. "Nudity on all beaches and public places with Lower Township is prohibited." Well, alrighty now. I park my bike and follow the path to the sea. Higbees is very au natural and secluded. It is, in fact, a meditation to sit on the beach and watch nature go by.

I feel calm and collected and am ready to head back to the chaos of a busy shoretown and, I have to say, very thankful that I live in a place where just five miles away a retreat from everyday life awaits me.

Susan Tischler is a staff writer for CapeMay.com and is also a co-owner of the Kaleidoscope boutique and the Shirt Outlet in Cape May.

Feet First
Words can barely describe how beautiful it is to walk
the beach to the lighthouse, but Susan Tischler tries

"CAR free/Care free" is the motto of a recent map published by
the West Cape May Citizens for Good Government. Produced
in an effort to encourage visitors and residents to park their
cars and leave them parked, the map is available at the Visitor
and Transportation Center of Cape May at Lafayette Street
(across from the Acme Grocery Store). So, I decided to give it a
go one Monday morning.

It's 8am and it looks like a great day for a walk. I jump out of

bed, get myself together and go to the Lemon Tree Restaurant on the Washington Street Mall for a proper Southern breakfast to send me on my way. I am not walking who knows how many miles on an empty stomach. After a glass of freshly squeezed orange juice, a cup of hot tea and a breakfast special with grits, I am on my way. One thing you should know - on any given day in the summer there are any number of walking tours available. Most of them are sponsored by the Mid-Atlantic Center for the Arts (MAC). Details and tickets are available at the information booth at the end of the Washington Street Mall.

Today, however, we'll do a little exploring of our own. The town isn't that big - you can basically walk from one end to the

To the lighthouse – not as far as it looks. *Photo: Susan Tischler/CapeMay.com*

other in 20 minutes. I turn down Decatur and head toward the beach. I cross Beach Avenue and step up on to the promenade. This is a great way to get in a walk and a view of the ocean all at the same time and today is a perfect day for walking on the promenade because it isn't as crowded as it is on the weekends. I head west toward the Cove beach and the end of the promenade but when I get to the end, it is such a beautiful, glistening morning that I figure, what the heck. I'm feeling all pumped up from those carbs I had for breakfast, so I step down on to the sand (this is the spot on the beach where many couples tie the knot) and I begin walking toward the lighthouse and Cape May Point.

I wish I were a poet at this moment because then I could describe how truly beautiful this morning is. Not to beat you over the head or anything, but you do have to walk the walk in order to experience it. Biking out to the Point is marvelous but not serene. All this – the clear sky, the pristine beach – it's like a scene from a movie. There is a nature trail leading from the beach to Cape May Point State Park. Now, you could continue on and you end up at Sunset Beach, but I decide to veer off, again heading toward the lighthouse. I walk just a little way on the nature path and I find myself in front of the Bird Observation Deck (another great place to get married, by the way). The lighthouse is just across the parking lot. I trudge over, and stand at the bottom of the lighthouse looking up.

I can't bear the thought of climbing those 199 steps leading to the top and sharing that narrow staircase with some portly man who tells me to get out the way because he's having an anxiety attack, or maybe it was vertigo, I can't remember. Don't get me wrong I've obviously done the lighthouse thing. Definitely worth the trip, particularly the night tour – wow! Heavenly. But, it's about 90 degrees and I would recommend the lighthouse thing late in the afternoon, when the air is cooler and the light in the sky is picture perfect.

Here's the other thing – I have to walk back. I could end this piece by telling you what a refreshing return trip I had; how I took my time and had a dip in the ocean. Don't tell anyone but I called my estranged husband and asked him if he'd come collect me in his pickup truck. And God bless him. That's just what he did. So – the moral of the story? Don't overshoot your energy level. Bring water, which I didn't. And always have a back-up plan.

Susan Tischler is a staff writer for CapeMay.com and is also a co-owner of the Kaleidoscope boutique and the Shirt Outlet in Cape May.

In Search of Davey's Lake
Follow Curtis Bashaw on a magical mystery
tour down by Higbees Beach

There is a lovely walk that I take at least a dozen or so times a year.
The feeling hits me, usually late in the afternoon when the sun is a
certain way. (It doesn't matter what season.) And so I am off. So
close, yet a world away.

Sometimes I go alone with my walking stick. Most often it
is with my niece and nephew. Other times it is with a posse of
friends and family. It feels like an expedition. It is always magical.

Davey's Lake is tucked away in the Higbees Beach Wildlife
Management Area, just behind the dune line. You can either drive
or bike to the end of New England Road and begin the trek from
the southwest corner of the dirt parking lot. (During the summer
months parking can be difficult – and the bike ride from town is
only about 15 minutes.)

The walk I like to do is my own combination of marked trails.
The park has trails sporadically marked by large posts with painted
tops. The loop beginning to end can take anywhere from 45 to
90 minutes, depending on whether you are on a march or a stroll.

Davey's Lake on an early morning in March. *Photo: Zoey Sless-Kitain*

THE GREAT OUTDOORS

The mystery Corvair.
Photo: Zoey Sless-Kitain

What is wonderful is that you see woodlands, farmlands and beach scapes, each beautiful in its own way.

Start at the southwest corner of the lot and look for the yellow trail marker. If you don't have a walking stick, look for one. That was my ritual until my dad gave me one he picked up at Orvis. After a few minutes you will come to a fork in the trail where the blue and yellow trails combine – head left here. You will know you are off in the right direction when you come quickly upon an old rusting Corvair. I tell my niece and nephew that their uncle drove that car there "back in the day", but that really isn't true. Each year there is less and less of the car. I am glad to see that no one has yet stolen the light-blue steering wheel.

The beginning is wooded but fairly quickly starts to merge with sand dunes. At the next fork you go left, heading due south. Depending on winds and surf you can hear the bay. The trail becomes increasingly sandy and hilly. In summer watch for poison ivy by the trail – it's everywhere in this section. You will come into an open sandy area – follow the blue trail here up a dune and down into the woods. These woods are lovely, filled with scrub oak, holly and cedar. As it gets lower and deeper you can smell and feel the softness of the place. There are beautiful lichens growing on fallen trees. As you wander the meandering trail you will invariably come to Mole Hollow, an area where the ground is soft and spongy because of the mole trails buried beneath.

Past the hollow the woods thicken a bit and become taller. There are lots of vines hanging from some walnut trees here. One vine in particular is a favorite of my nephew. We always stop and he climbs and swings. (Please test them first.)

Just after the swinging vine the trail becomes imperceptible. Don't fret, just keep forging ahead. This part of the trail has an abundance of wild roses and brambles. The thorns are intimidating – but they don't last long and you can pick your way through. At the end you break through into a lovely farm field.

When you reach the field you basically head south, or to the right. The first field ends quickly at a small lane. This takes you through to the second field. There are wildflowers mingled in with vestiges of the old crops - lima beans or corn. At the end of the second field take the lane through to the third. Continue south to the end of the third field. This takes you to a long lane with ivy on both sides and some massive oaks, holly and cedars. You can hear mourning doves or owls or woodpeckers. It reminds me of Robert Frost's poem "The Road Less Traveled".

Towards the end of the long lane you will see a sandy, sunny area. We call this Toad Hall. If you are quiet you can sneak up on them. From May through October they are almost always there, sunning themselves in the sand. Toad Hall marks the end of the wood and farmlands and the beginning of the desert landscape. This is the trickiest part of the walk. The blue trail has been lost and you pick up an orange one. Eventually you come into a large sandy area. Stay to the middle, walking past a quartet of junipers on the left. At the end of summer their berries are a beautiful blue/grey (I fantasize that there is a hidden treasure chest of gin underneath). Past the junipers, it seems as if the trail is lost. Just keep going, leaning right. You will start to feel the pull of Davey's Lake.

This area looks like a scene from *Mad Max* or something. There is a holly clump on the left, and then a very large sprawling shrub that just seems to emanate from the dune itself. Davey's Lake is just over the hill, but to protect the dunes please turn right and look for the orange stakes again. Head west to where the orange and blue stakes meet. Here you go left. You will walk past sprawling beach plums, scraggly sticks in the winter, late bloomers in spring, laden every Labor Day with tart little plums from which a wonderful jam can be made.

This is how I discovered the place. My grandfather loved to drag us out on Labor Day weekend to pick beach plums. Even though he is gone we still do it and most years we get some jam into jars.

When you find Davey's Lake you should also find the pair of swans that have been its keepers for years. It is so lovely here – walk around, sit down, unzip your backpack and have a drink of water. If you happen to get there for the gloaming, that time of day when the setting sunlight just makes everything, well, gloam, you will most certainly sigh and smile and be happy.

I like to return via the bay. I go back to the orange and blue

Driftwood at magical Higbees.
Photo: Zoey Sless-Kitain

stake, walk another 30 paces north and then turn west to the bay. There is a path, more beach plum and juniper bushes and some wonderful scrub oak and pine. You feel the wind of the bay and then you are at the beach.

I always take my shoes off here, roll up my pants and let the saltwater get rid of any poison ivy that might have rubbed off along the way. To the left is the sunken ship at Sunset Beach. To the right is the blue dome of the ferry terminal – walk toward that. On the way, pick up some water-washed pebbles and watch sandpipers scarpering around – in June there are the horseshoe crabs. Eventually you will come to the voodoo tree. Say a prayer that the dunes will keep hold and that there won't be much more erosion (and don't steal any driftwood). One hundred and eighty-five paces after the voodoo tree, turn into the dunes and follow the trail to the parking lot.

I hope you enjoyed the walk and that you left the place as you found it.

Curtis Bashaw is joint managing partner of Congress Hall in Cape May and executive director of the Casino Reinvestment Development Authority.

A Flying Lesson

You think birding is just for the geeks? Susan Tischler did, then she spent a dazzling evening on the water.

One night I took a sunset Salt Marsh Safari on "The Skimmer," a 40 ft. pontoon which skims the waterways just like the bird it was named for. Admittedly, I wouldn't have thought to go on it if I hadn't been on an assignment. Why? Because birding is a huge component of the safari and birders intimidate me.

First, it's about the equipment. Birders always have the tools at their disposal to see the birds. I do not have the tools. I do not have a pair of powerful Leika or Swarovski binoculars. So, already I'm out of the loop. Also, they know what to look for when someone yells "Hey, American Oyster Catcher at 11 o'clock." Where? I ask myself. Where's the clock? What clock? Wait, I see it's an imaginary clock. Okay. So, 11 o'clock is what – right or left? I imagine hundreds of clocks. All of them digital. I follow the body language of veteran birders just like any stranger in a strange land who doesn't understand the language, but to no avail. By the time I figure out where I'm supposed to be looking, the bird has gone. While everyone else is ooing and

A merlin at Cape May Point. *Photo: Richard Crossley*

aahing, I'm groaning and moaning.

I have to say, though, that Captain Bob Carlough and his able assistant and wife Linda Carlough put me at ease immediately. They bought equipment. I had, for the two hours we were skimming the wetlands, my own set of powerful binoculars. They even have kid-size binoculars. Secondly, they explained the o'clock thing by pointing. The front of the boat is 12 o'clock. The back of the boat is 6 o'clock. Each side is... well you get it I'm sure. Also note they didn't do that boater's thing either because had they said the bow or the stern of the boat my head would still be swimming around like something out of *The Exorcist*.

Like any good teacher, Captain Bob is a strong believer in show and tell. The South Jersey wetlands are, he says, "more fertile than the Amazon." It is the beginning of the food chain, he says, and by way of example he has a basin filled with food sources for birds and the ecosystem in general. He pulls out a tiny glass shrimp and a beautiful thumb-sized crab called the Savory Swimmer with wee paddles for back legs. He has a sample of an equally small walking crab.

Once The Skimmer is out of the dock and winding its way through the canal toward the Coast Guard Base, the bird watch alert is up. The sightings are plentiful.

"Heron at 11 o'clock," says Linda Carlough. Okay. I'm still a little slow with the o'clock thing but I'm able to follow everyone else and thank the gods these birds are big and white. Even I spot the heron, as well as the great egret, snowy egret, black skimmer, and the great blue heron. Ahhh. At last I can sit back and relax. My next source of anxiety is that I've traded my bin-

A sanderling at Two-mile beach, Wildwood Crest. *Photo: Richard Crossley*

oculars for my Nikon digital camera, when this was definitely a time for the 35 mm Nikon with the zoom lens because guess what? You have to be pretty quick on the trigger to get a really nice picture of a bird in flight, or when it's getting ready to pounce on something. Another problem is that my digital zoom is not zoomy enough to close in (especially while the boat is in motion) on the green eyes of the cormorants. So I put the camera away for a while and go back to the binoculars which are fabulous. Best to leave the photographs to the professionals.

Captain Bob points to an osprey nest with three chicks in it. He is very excited about seeing the nest because he said the harsh winter ice took its toll on the wetlands' grasses and there haven't been as many successful nests this summer. However, because of the passage of the Clean Water Act as well as the Wetlands Restoration Acts, and similar ecologically friendly legislation, life in the back bays has seen quite a transformation. There were, he said, only 50 osprey pairs in 1972. Last year 340 were cited.

Meanwhile, the Skimmer pulls up to a long blanket of green algae floating on the water and comes to a stop so we can get a closer look at this wonder of nature.

We step out on to what I call the front porch of the pontoon which is level with the patch. Captain Bob skims a seaweed called Mermaid Hair from the water. Linda explains that it is called Mermaid Hair because it looks like someone's head of hair when it floats in the water. Before we leave we see blood worms and many birds. This patch is like a feeding trough for birds. A semi-palmated plover, a black-bellied plover, and a ruddy turnstone were having their evening repast, not to mention the American oyster catcher.

As the boat swings around, we don't go very far before we are in the thick of the salt marsh. I can see Wildwood Crest at 3 o'clock and a thick colony of long, green reed-like growth.

"The Salt Marsh," said Captain Bob, "is the most bio-productive ecosystem in the world." Because of the way everything works back here – the reeds separating the salt from the ocean water and crystallizing it, the peat that forms the land mass on which the reeds can grow, and the rich fertile environment which results – all these components come together to create "the beginning of the food chain of the ocean." And to prove his point, Captain Bob grabs a chunk of peat to show us not only

A Cape May warbler at the Bird Observatory. *Photo Richard Crossley*

the richness of the soil but also the millions of micro-organisms which live in it. "Life," he says, "begins back here with the micro-organisms that live here." The peat acts like a sponge for them and absorbs them.

I am struck by how beautiful the grasses are. They are a deep, lush green. They are thick and majestic. I want to run my hand through them just to a get a sense of what they feel like. As though reading my mind, Captain Bob encourages us to touch them. In other years, they can be broken off like stalks of salt, he says, but again the odd weather of the past couple of seasons makes them feel like softer and more pliable.

The Skimmer pulls around to what looks like an island on which a mad scientist would live. Tall, gangly trees have grown there and it is thick with greenery and very weird. It's a heron

Sanderling, dunlin and ruddy turnstone at Two-mile Beach, Wildwood Crest.
Photo: Richard Crossley

rookery. I can't believe it! Hundreds of giant birds – blue herons, osprey, egrets are checking in for the night. This is their hotel. Captain Bob says some 600 birds (just a guess, he admits) will spend the night there. He says they fly in squadrons of 10-12 until it gets dark. Right now, he estimates there are only about 75 great birds.

And on top of the trees, above the herons and egrets, whose plumage forms pockets of snowy white against a darkening sky and mossy green growth, are hundreds of black crows menacingly perched, looking as though they're waiting for any sign of weakness so they can pounce. Captain Bob says they coexist pretty well with the other birds. Maybe the herons have hired them as sentinels, placed there to guard them while they sleep. It is just about the coolest thing I've ever seen.

The sun really is setting now and The Skimmer begins its

journey back to the Miss Chris Marina, though there are still things to see in between the 150 pictures of the sunset that I compulsively keep taking. There are a couple of fishermen out in their boats still trying to get the catch of the day. They look so peaceful against the night sky and I think of Ernest Hemingway's *The Old Man and the Sea* – not that they were that old, but the waters have turned suddenly cold and they look so small and vulnerable in comparison with the large fishing boats docked behind them.

As we pass under the Cape May bridge, Linda Carlough reminds us that we and our children (and by the way I highly recommend this voyage for children, particularly those, say, eight and up) are the caretakers of the land and "I hope," she says, "we will have the wisdom that it takes to make us good stewards" and to continue to protect nature's precious gift to us.

The Salt Marsh Safari is truly something different for you to do with your family or even by yourself while you're vacationing in Cape May. Hey, even if you live here this is not the usual tourist tripe. (Not that there's anything wrong with tripe. Tripe is nothing less than a good thing-turned-snoozer when you've seen it or done it a hundred times.)

The Skimmer leaves from the Miss Chris Marina on 2nd Avenue & Wilson Drive. There's a Morning Refuge Cruise at 10 a.m., an afternoon Osprey Odyssey at 1:30 p.m. and the Sunset on the Marsh cruise at 6 p.m. The sunset cruise runs Sunday through Thursday, but check out the website at www.skimmer.com first for reservations and schedule changes.

This piece originally appeared on CapeMay.com.

CHAPTER TWO
Magic Moments

It's the Little Things...

Twenty one in-a-nutshell experiences that should make your Cape May stay a memorable one

YOU can spend a lot of time trying to plan the perfect vacation (indeed, we offer our own thoughts on that in the next chapter), but often it's the little things that really swing it – the moments that, taken together, add up to something quite special. Let's call these Magic Moments, which, not accidentally, is the heading for this chapter.

We've assembled a collection of what we think are must-do Cape May experiences. We should say now that the vast majority of them involve food or alcohol or both, but we're not ashamed of that, and neither should you be. So sit back, relax and don't get the yellow highlighter pen out or anything, because that would spoil the book, but you might want to select your favorites from this chapter and make up your list of things you just have to do. Then again, you might not.

1. The word "enchanting" is not one that regular folks usually use in conversation, but it's just the right word to describe the moonlight trolley ride to Cape May's lighthouse or, as the

Stairway to the stars – the lighthouse by moonlight. *Photo by MAC*

MAGIC MOMENTS

Mid-Atlantic Center for the Arts calls it, the **Stairway to the Stars** tour. First, you buys your ticket at the kiosk at Washington Street Mall and then you gets your butt on the trolley and sit and sigh and purr with contentment as it wends its way down Beach Avenue, down Broadway and then along Sunset Boulevard (this being one of the most memorable drives around) to the Cape May Lighthouse. Tour guides will tell you about the history of Cape May's famous beacon, though if you're one of the many young laddies who have popped the big question to their lassie at the top of the lighthouse then at this stage you'll be sweating and fretting rather than listening. So, anyway, then you'll climb the lighthouse's 199 steps to the watch gallery, where the navy blue sky ablaze with stars engulfs you. Gaze at the moon, kiss your lover, or the nearest person to you (honestly, it's fine), as you overlook the Atlantic Ocean, glittering and reflecting the night sky's light. If the rest of your marriage is as good as this moment, then you will be truly blessed. The tour begins at 8pm and runs on Tuesday, Thursday and Saturday nights in the summer.

2. Perch on a bar stool or sit back on the rich chocolate-brown velvet chairs in **The Brown Room**, Congress Hall cocktail lounge, at around 9pm on a Friday night and listen to the smoky jazz of Lois Smith and the Johnny Andrews Trio.

3. It's kind of like *American Idol* meets the Civil War, and taking part in the strange phenomenon called Terrible Tuesday in the **Ugly Mug**, Cape May's oldest-surviving bar, is a must. Starting around midnight, the bar splits into two as customers decide whether to join the South Side or the North Side in a singing contest that always – and only – features Neil Diamond's *Sweet*

MAGIC MOMENTS

Pitch battle – Terrible Tuesdays at the Ugly Mug. *Photo: Maciej Nabrdalik*

Caroline. Customers are encouraged to stand on stools/tables/shoulders as they take their shot at outsinging the other side. The winning side gets served 50-cent pints of beer.

4. At around 5.30pm on a sunny summer day, grab two bikes (don't steal them – rent or bring your own), grab your partner, friend, colleague, grandmother, mistress, slaveboy (don't steal them either – bring your own) and cycle all the way down Lafayette Street, starting at Collier's Liquor Store, over the little Cape May bridge, hang a right when you see the big sign for the Lobster House, lock up your bikes and saunter toward the **Schooner American,** which is permanently docked at the harbor, as an add-on to the main Lobster House restaurant. Head for the bow-shaped bar, sit down and order two smashing drinks – the

Hang a right for a memorable margarita experience. *Photo: Stephen Spagnuola*

margaritas are particularly good – and sip them as you watch the hustle and bustle of the harbor. Down here it's a different kind of Cape May – like you just walked on to the set of *Jaws* (without the man-eating shark, of course). The Schooner is one of the top three places for outdoor cocktails in Cape May (to discover the others, just keep reading the book).

5. At around 4pm on a warm summer or fall day, make the beautiful walk down fragrant Washington Street. Go past the glorious Southern Mansion and just before the also-glorious Emlen Physick Estate, walk into the **William J. Moore Tennis Club**, make for the clubhouse, go in and announce grandly, "Exit Zero sent me. Now where are my damn balls and rackets?" Alternatively, just nicely ask that you'd like to rent a court. Then whack some balls around for an hour, work up a goodly sweat (but not so much that you'll scare the horses) and then allow it to dry off as you walk back up Washington, pausing to admire the beautiful homes that line this old street. By the time you hit the center of town again, you'll be ready for an ice-cold beer, which tastes SO good after a hot game of tennis. Take your pick – the Ugly Mug, Pilot House and Jackson Mountain Café are all in the mall, or head for the beach, to Carney's or Cabanas. After your second beer (don't overdo it), head home, take a lukewarm shower, feel the bite of the water against your sunburned skin, change into cool cottons and anticipate a mellow evening of eating and drinking.

6. At 5pm on a summer Sunday, walk over to the Chalfonte Hotel's **King Edward Bar** on Howard Street – they have a beautiful display of imported cheeses and other goodies from DiBruno Bros in Philly. It's an impressive spread, and it's free. Take a sampling of everything there, get a nice glass of merlot (not free), and sit at one of the cozy tables or on the side porch and you're in heaven. This is a popular locals' spot so you're sure to meet some interesting folks. After you've nibbled (the food, not the locals), go to the hotel's Magnolia Room restaurant. They have a Sunday Southern Supper Buffet from 6-9 pm. Make sure you call a few days ahead for reservations. The buffet has all the Chalfonte's signature items, notably their fried chicken which has won acclaim all over the country for decades. After you've stuffed yourself, go to the front porch and park yourself in one of the 30 or so rockers and watch the world go by while you digest. If you've timed this right, you'll be on the porch around sunset, and if you step off the

Cosmos at the Pelican Club, courtesy of Mark Kane. *Photo: Jack Wright*

porch and look up at the hotel from the sidewalk, you'll see the whole top half of the hotel turn pink from the reflection of her red roofs.

7. About an hour before sunset, walk over to Beach Avenue & Decatur Street and into the lobby of the Marquis De Lafayette hotel. Keep going past the front desk and over to the elevators. Go to the 6th floor to **The Pelican Club**. As you step off the elevator, you'll see a rather large carved Pelican – pat its tail for good luck. Go to the large oval bar and grab two stools facing the ocean. From there, you'll see a beautiful sunset, but this is also the time when you might see small schools of dolphin feeding fairly close to the shoreline. If you like Bloody Marys, Pelican Club makes the best in town. Instead of eating in the dining room, you could order apps and dinner right there at the bar. Definitely appetizers – their spring rolls are divine, as are the salad of ripe tomatoes layered with baby arugula and goat cheese with a balsamic vinaigrette.

8. In the early afternoon, make a reservation at **Waters Edge** for, say, 8pm. At around 6.30, make your way from the center of town and stroll all the way down the promenade (hand in hand, preferably, unless you have serious intimacy issues). After a distance of a mile or so (it's good for you), cross the road when you see the big motel, Le Mer. Just in front of that, on the corner of Beach and Pittsburgh, sits a much smaller building – that would be the Waters Edge. Head straight for the bar (hopefully there will be a seat for you and yours) and shoot the breeze with bartender Gary LaRue (as always, we recommend you namedrop *Exit Zero* here – it goes a long way). Order a Manhattan or maybe a Stoli and tonic and stare out to the ocean as the dolphins and whales

Gary LaRue shakes his thang at Waters Edge. *Photo: Stephen Spagnuola*

cavort in the surf – okay so you won't be able to see any dolphins or whales, but after a couple of Gary's Manhattans, you could probably convince yourself you did. And then have dinner at one of the best restaurants in south Jersey.

9. At around 6am, make your way down to the beach and walk along the promenade. After a nice walk, go up Ocean Street where there are a number of B&Bs. There's always activity – walks being swept, early risers on the porches, flags being hung in the fronts of the old Victorians, and along this stretch up to Washington, you'll inhale all the wonderful smells of the B&B kitchens – muffins, bacon, fresh coffee. Make your way over to the WaWa on Bank Street, pick up a copy of the *New York Times* and then walk back to the mall to **The Lemon Tree**. It's bustling at any hour, and it's a watering hole for locals and merchants, so the earlier you get there, the better chance you have to get a window seat. Order at the counter – the fresh-squeezed OJ is a treat, the home fries are delicious, and Fred's Benedict is pure sin. This is a perfect spot for people-watching, which will serve mostly to distract you from even trying to read the paper, but it'll make you look intelligent and interesting as it sits on the table.

10. Cocktail hour is a great thing. There's something just so civilized about getting on your best white pants, Ralph Lauren polo, sandals and settling down for a quiet cocktail at 6.30pm, just before dinner. And then there's Happy Hour at **Cabanas**, which is somewhat different. Cabanas is on the beachfront, on the corner of Decatur, and is one of the livelier places in town. In season, their floor-to-ceiling windows open up, making for a quite refreshing and inspiring place in which to imbibe half-price drinks from 4-

A magical misty morning on the beachfront. *Photo: Mary Pat Myers*

7pm. Okay, so it might mess up the dinner plans you had for later, but you're on vacation, so what's the problem here?

11. If you like to bump 'n' grind with hot young Jersey girls – and boys – to the sounds of a poppy cover band on a sultry summer night, make for Carney's, at Beach and Jackson. If you value personal space, decent conversation and lots of fresh air, then come here in the daytime only. On a lively night, Carney's is the kind of place that sweeps you in the front door then propels you through a rollicking rollercoaster of a night which leaves you with your ears ringing, your legs wobbling and if you're really lucky... okay, we won't go there.

12. Elsewhere in this book we mention Terrible Tuesday, the raucously-fun night that the Ugly Mug runs in season. Well, for an entirely different Tuesday evening in Cape May, there's **The Merion Inn**. If the Mug's Tuesdays are for those who are either young or pretend to be, then the Merion's Tuesdays are for those who are a little more mature or pretend to be, or just grew up before their time. We're talking jazz fans. Jazz fans who like to listen to a master like George Mesterhazy work his magic on the baby Grand while you stand at the Merion's charming old bar, sipping on a Bushmills or a Jameson's or a gin or tonic or whatever it is that mature jazz fans like to sip on. The Merion is on Decatur, a block from the beach. The food's really good, too. So if you're a jazz fan, book a table for eight and make a night of it. We probably should add here that every night is a good jazz night at the Merion, but for some reason the locals prefer to go on Tuesdays. We have no idea why this is.

13. It's 5pm, you've been on the beach all day and you Want. A. Refreshment. Right. Now. And you don't want to get dressed up. That's fine. Just shake the sand off your body, put your T-shirt on and cross Beach Avenue to the **Fin Bar**, on the corner of Decatur. The Fin Bar is the little cabana that sits beside the swimming pool at the Marquis de Lafayette. You can't actually jump in the pool, unless you're a hotel resident, but you can sit yourself at the bar, which has a tropical feel to it, and chug down a cold beer or two.

14. If you love architecture, history, gardening and daiquiris, you must promise yourself an afternoon at the pool cabana at **Congress Hall**. If there are many better ways to while away the day then we just haven't been paying attention. Congress Hall, in case you're a very new visitor and tend to stare at the ground when you walk, is the amazing big yellow building that sits on a lawn overlooking Beach Avenue. The hotel is a book in itself (and guess what, one exists, by this same publisher – what a coincidence!) but we'll keep it brief. Congress Hall was first built in 1816,

Congress Hall's pool cabana is a glorious spot for cocktails.
Photo: David Gray

making it the oldest seaside hotel in the country. It was twice destroyed by fire and the building that now stands dates from 1879. Anyway, to the point: even if you're not a resident, you can stroll over to the pool cabana and take a seat at the bar or at the tables that over-look the pool and marvel at the colonnade, the beautiful flowers and shrubs, at the ocean, at the beautiful people wearing white T-shirts with pink stars who serve you and at the colorful and tasty cocktails, complete with lots of lovely umbrellas and cherries.

15. See Cape May's official flower – the hydrangea – in full bloom in May and June at the **Emlen Physick Estate**. These 35-year-old bushes thrive in Cape May because of the acidic soil and high humidity. The glorious fragrant blooms feature every shade of purple, lavender, blue and periwinkle imaginable.

16. If you like to people watch as you eat, and you like to eat top-quality Italian food, reserve an outdoor table at **A Ca Mia,**

on Washington Street Mall, across from the old church. En route, stop off at Collier's, the big green liquor store on Perry Street and pick up some wine – like many Cape May restaurants, A Ca Mia is BYO. (By the way, have you ever seen someone turn up at a BYO and plonk a bottle of gin, a litre of tonic, a bunch of limes and a bag of ice on the table? It doesn't happen, does it? Sounds like an idea, though. Because, c'mon, not everybody drinks wine.) Anyway, if you're a man remember that it's important to give your lady friend the chair that looks on to the mall because it is a scientific fact that girls, and girlie men, like to people watch more than men, or manly girls. While we're on the subject of etiquette, it's rude and unlucky to sip from your drink without clinking glasses. Not every time, but definitely for the first drink of the night.

17. The British are not known for their food, but they did invent afternoon tea, one of the most civilized and tastiest traditions in the universe. Given that Cape May is a Victorian town, you might not be surprised (unless you didn't pay attention in school and didn't realize that the Victorian era originated in Britain – named after Queen Victoria in case you really didn't know this) to hear that it does a very good version of afternoon tea. (By the way,

Tea at Twinings. *Photo by MAC*

The hydrangea, Cape May's official plant. *Photo: Mary Pat Myers*

that previous sentence, with its long parenthetical clause, was a bit hard to swallow, and we can assure you – nay, promise you – that we'll steer clear of any more unnecessarily long sentences which cause you to take a deep breath, since, after all, this book is aimed at giving you a short and snappy guide to Cape May, the Victorian jewel of America – you still reading this?) Enjoy pistachio tea bread and orange-raisin scones smeared with clotted cream as you sip a steaming cup of your favorite Twinings Tea during an elegant afternoon tea at the Twinings Tearoom, located on the grounds of the Emlen Physick Estate. If it's a glorious day, sit on a bench by the garden, watch the birds and bunnies frolic in the grass (we trust that frolicking bunnies won't put you off your tea) as you imbibe the spirit of the Victorian era and let the afternoon slowly pass by. You might even want to take a nap. The Twinings Tearoom is open March-January.

18. If you need a break from Victorian Cape May but still want to experience the splendor of eating and drinking while staring at the sea, jump in your car and drive over the West Cape May bridge, up Bayshore Road, toward the ferry, then hang a right on Bay Road, where you go straight up until you reach **Harpoon Henry's**. You could imagine yourself in the Caribbean. That's the vibe of this place, situated as it is on the sparsely-populated Bay beach. It used to be called Whaler's Cove and it was always a fantastic place to enjoy cocktails and frozen drinks, but the food was often something of a disappointment. That should change now that the place is under the ownership of Ed and Teresa Henry, who also run Henry's on the Beach and Zoe's. These two know how to serve good quality food at decent prices (the two don't always go together in Cape May, as you might have noticed).

19. While we're on the subject of outdoor dining, the other great place in town is **Gecko's**, which occupies a totally cute little spot on Carpenter Street, across the road from Congress Hall. Gecko's has indoor tables, too, but in season, you'll want an outdoor berth. Everything about Gecko's is wonderful, from the food, which is southwestern/Mexican, to the staff, especially waiter Sean, who has wavy blond hair and a smile that just won't quit. We recommend bringing along a six-pack of Corona to start, with a fruity red or white to follow, and kicking back while the boys and girls of Gecko's make you smile.

20. Walking through Cape May's Historic District is a blast – so many styles of homes, so many glorious little details and charming, tree-lined streets. But if you're not as fit as you'd like to be (or are perhaps a *homo sapien lazyassius*) or just like to ride trolleys, jump aboard one of the red and green trolleys operated by MAC, not the makeup store but the Mid-Atlantic Center for

A glorious full moon over the Atlantic. *Photo: Maciej Nabrdalik*

the Arts, who pretty much saved Cape May back in the 1970s. Look to the left and right as you get the inside scoop on Cape May's cupolas, belvederes, convex and concave Mansard roofs, Italianates, colonials, Queen Annes, stick styles and more. And if you don't know what these are, then get on the trolley already! Discover the town's one and only mother-in-law porch, learn which famous inn has so many different design styles that it's believed the architect was a drunk, and spot the house with the upside-down chimneys. Then during dinner spout the Victorian facts you learned while on the half-hour tour and impress your pals.

21. Finally, just take a little time to stare at the moon glowing over the Atlantic. The lifeguard seats offer a wonderful view, as our photo shows, though this being-on-the-beach-after-dark experience will cost you $65 – make checks payable to City of Cape May. Still, it *is* a pretty photo.

CHAPTER THREE
Perfect Days

We Want to Make You Happy

Six itineraries for couples and families that we hope will make you very, very contented vacationers

FIRST of all, let's just agree that there is no such thing as a perfect day. Just as there's no such thing as a perfect vacation and anyone who tells you otherwise is deluded and most likely had a much less than perfect vacation. However, it makes a snappy chapter heading and anyway there IS such a thing as a day that's constructed out of so many good components that it's as close as you're going to get, especially when kids (or marriages) are involved.

As well as detailing our own Itineraries From Heaven, we also asked the opinions of a random assortment of local people, from the fire chief, to bartenders, restaurant owners and the like. We hope you'll find our and their suggestions helpful.

Perfect Day for a Couple #1

ON the eve of your perfect day, perform the following tasks: 1. Rent bikes with baskets for you and your honey if you don't already have one (a bike, not a honey – we're assuming you have that covered already); 2. Call **Tisha's** restaurant (884-9119), behind Convention Hall and ask for a table for two at 6.30pm,

Poverty Beach, at the east end of town, feels mystical. *Photo: Jim Cheney*

on the outside decking, overlooking the beach. The next morning, get up at 8am, get on your bike and cycle to the **WaWa** on Bank Street. Get your large coffees, sausage & egg muffins and some tubs of fresh fruit. Then make the short ride to one of the benches on the boardwalk. Pick a perch and try not to feel so bad when you munch into your muffin as yet another jogger goes by. After all, you'll be biking a few miles today, so you'll be fine. When you're done, you're going to take the ride described on page 30. You should be done around 10am.

Now you should ride to the north end of Beach Avenue to **Poverty Beach**, where you should settle and snooze and read at this beautiful little stretch of sand. At noon, head back to your hotel/B&B/inn/motel/trailer/tent, drop off your bikes and get the car. Then go on Broadway, heading north. Go over the West

MY PERFECT DAY
Anne LeDuc, owner Chalfonte Hotel

I'D GET up early enough to see the sun rise over the ocean. I like to go to a couple different beaches, starting on Howard. Then I'd hurry back to take a friend with me to birdwatch at the Point. I'm not an ardent birdwatcher, but it's a nice activity. Then I'd come back and have a wonderful buffet breakfast at the Chalfonte with my favorites of spoon bread and home-made biscuits, chipped beef and eggs, with lots of fresh fruit. After, I'd go out and rock on the front porch with the *Philadelphia Inquirer* for a little while around 9:30am to settle my breakfast. Then I'd head for Washington Street Mall. I'm not much of a shopper but I like to look at clothes or gifts for friends, especially Cape May memorabilia. Then I'd walk back, admiring the Victorian architecture. I'm still amazed after, I won't even tell you how many years, by how beautiful this town is. Then I'd go back to the Howard beach. I'm not a beach person that likes to lie in the sun – I like to stand and watch the waves and get my ankles wet. Then I'd have a tuna sandwich and clam chowder at one of the outside restaurants. I love to nap in the afternoon, so I'd do that then drive to Cape May National and hit some golf balls. I'd get back around 6pm, in time to rest and dress for dinner. First, I'd go down to the King Edward bar here at the Chalfonte and have a glass of wine or a tropical drink, then I'd go to a restaurant like the Pelican Club, Washington Inn or Congress Hall. If we have a cabaret at the Chalfonte, I'd catch some of that before retiring. I'm an early-to-bedder – I love to lie and listen to the horse-drawn carriages clanking up the street.

The rugged charm of Higbees Beach. *Photo: Zoey Sless-Kitain*

Cape May Bridge. When you get to the second set of lights after the bridge, Townbank Road, make a left and after a mile or so, you'll find the **Cape May Winery** on your right. Spend some time sampling the magnificent wine collection and browse the little gift shop. Don't overdo the sampling because that's not the only vineyard you're going to be visiting. When you exit, go right and then left on 644 (Shunpike Road). Go across Sandman and then right on 603 (Bayshore). Look for a soccer field on your right and then you'll see a cream-colored Italian-style villa. This is the home of **Turdo Vineyards**, run by a sweet Sicilian couple called Salvatore and Sara Turdo. Enjoy some meats and cheeses as you sample their North Cape May wines, which include award-winning Merlot and Pinot Grigio. After you've decided on which bottles you're going to take home with you, get back in the car and go back over the bridge. About a mile after you cross, you'll

see a little fruit stand called **Duckie's Market** on your right. Stop and get some fresh fruit – you're going for a little picnic on the beach. Now turn back around and go left on 645 (aka Stimpson Lane, which happens to be the home of *Exit Zero*), go right when you get to the junction of 604 (Bayshore), then go left when you hit New England. Follow that all the way until you hit the dead end which is the **Higbees Beach** parking lot. Follow the path that takes you to the beach and settle down to enjoy your fruit and favorite beverage. Naturally, you'll know that it's illegal to bring alcohol on to the beach, just in case you were thinking about packing a couple of nice glasses in the car with you and enjoying a glass of Cape May wine on this secluded and romantic stretch of sand.

After a mid-afternoon nap on the beach and a dip in the ocean, you're ready to head back to your room. It's about 4pm and first of all you need to call a cab (see the A-Z), to book a car for your 6.30pm reservation at **Tisha's**, situated behind Convention Hall, right on the beach. The seafood and steaks were described as "extraordinary" by the 2003 Zagat. You'll be finishing your dessert as the sun starts its glorious descent and then you'll be off to catch the 8pm showing of **Cape May Stage**'s performance of *Stones in His Pockets* (June 30-Aug 14), which won Best Comedy in London's Olivier Awards. Call Cape May Stage at (609) 884-1341 for tickets.

After that, you'll be tired, but a stroll back along the boardwalk, under the stars, should be attempted before you go home.

This is the view from your parasail perch. *Photo: Maciej Nabrdalik*

If your stamina is up for it, finish your day with a nightcap at Congress Hall's **Brown Room**, as elegant a cocktail lounge as you'll find for miles around. Lovely though the interior is, you've had a long day so take your drinks outside on to the veranda and settle into the rocking chairs that overlook the lawn, the illuminated swimming pool (aren't swimming pool lights so cool?) and the ocean. You might even fall asleep right there. G'night.

Perfect Day for a Couple #2

THIS day is going to be centered around the beach area, so again, a nice, clear day is important. And, again, you're going to be on your bikes for most of this day. Get up around 8ish, and have breakfast at **Zoe's Beachfront Eatery**, on Beach Avenue, right next to the theater. After that, get on Lafayette or Washington and go over the little Cape May bridge, heading

MY PERFECT DAY
Dave Ellenberg, Executive Director, Cape May Chamber of Commerce

I'D GET up at 6 o'clock, have my coffee and read the paper a little bit. Then I'd be on my way to Cape May National and play 18 holes. I'd get changed then take in an early afternoon lunch at one of the local pubs along the beachfront. From there I'd head to the little information booth on the Washington Street Mall and take a horse and carriage ride. It shows the Victorian homes and Victorian areas of Cape May. It's about a half an hour trip and one of the guides, Beverly, gives a particularly great tour. Then I'd take a little walk around town, starting on Ocean Street and taking a left on Columbia. I'd walk up a few blocks to where the Abbey is then take a right turn and walk to the beach. Making my way back I'd circle around to the mall to do some antique, jewelry, or candy shopping. Then I'd take in happy hour at a pub right there. Later, I'd get changed and eat dinner at any of the excellent restaurants that we have in Cape May. From there, I would take in a late show. I love Jilline Ringle's cabaret show at the Chalfonte Hotel. By then I'd be ready for bed but I might take in an after-dinner drink if I was feeling up to it.

toward the Parkway. As you go over the bridge you'll see a sign for South Jersey Marina on your right before the Lobster House. Pull in, lock your bike and find **Pegleg Parasail**. You will already have made a reservation at least a day before, for 10am (898-1600). When you call, tell them you want to go up together as a couple and they'll fix you up with a harness made for two. The only exception to this is if your combined weight would make it too tricky, so be prepared to tell them that number (and don't eat too many pancakes at Zoe's beforehand). You'll then be taken on a lovely little boat trip out to the ocean where you will then be hoisted 500 feet up in the air. Please don't be afraid. This is not extreme sports. You will most likely feel a little chicken at first, but there's no need. Pegleg go to great lengths to keep their equipment totally safe. When you're up there, you'll be glad you

The feast is about to begin at Daniel's. *Photo: Stephen Spagnuola*

made the effort. The view is fantastic and the feeling is glorious. Once you've come back down to earth, get back on your bikes and ride to the Cove beach, nap, read, nap, read, play paddle ball, dip in the ocean, then one of you should get back on the bike and ride up to the **Akroteria**, a collection of little beach shacks that sell excellent cheesesteaks, hot dogs and other carb-filled treats (you're on vacation). Eat, nap, read, nap, dip in the ocean and then you'll be ready for action again at around 4pm.

Ride up to the **Arcade**, where you'll both play skee ball and attempt to win a fluffy toy for whoever in your relationship likes these kinds of things. Of course, the average player would have to play for around four days, around the clock, to muster enough points to get a little teddy. More likely, you'll win a plastic bracelet that you can inscribe your honey's name on. By the way, trying, like we did, to buy one of the cuddly toys with cold, hard cash won't wash, sadly.

After this thorough workout, it'll be time for a cool beer, and for that you only have to walk across the road to either **Carney's** or **Cabanas**.

At about 6pm, go back to your room, freshen up, watch some junk TV on the WB, slip into your cool, white cottons and walk, or cab, to **Daniel's on Broadway**. Last year, the Food Network voted Daniel's one of the top five BYO restaurants in the country. You'll see why – the food is sensational and the ambience delightful. When you make your reservation (and we recommend at least a day ahead), ask for the back room, which was originally a whalers' kitchen/living-room and which dates from the mid-1700s.

Play for hours, win a bracelet. *Photo: Maciej Nabrdalik*

After that, make your way to **The Boiler Room**, the basement club in Congress Hall. They recently renovated the place, both in terms of the music and the decor. Now it's open seven nights a week, playing mostly cool, sexy jazz and loungey music. Perfect for a chilled-out evening to finish up your perfect day.

Perfect Rainy Day for a Couple

FIRST of all, stay in bed until around 10am and get in some extra lovin', or sleeping, or, better still, breakfast in bed if your particular place has that little luxury. If you're staying in a place that doesn't serve breakfast, grab a booth at the **Lobster House** coffee shop or **George's Place** on Beach and Perry. Read the paper, sip an extra cup of coffee and remember what you realize when you're in an airplane — a cloudy day is exactly the same as a sunny day at 35,000 feet. It's all blue and wonderful; it's just that sometimes

MY PERFECT DAY
Corey Gilbert, owner Tides of Time Gallery

IT WOULD begin an hour before sunrise, when my wife Angela and I would head over to the north end of town and watch the sun rise at Poverty Beach. There's usually some fishermen up there. From there, we would go to George's Place, which has a great breakfast. Then we'd check out some of the latest stuff at the beachfront shops, find some toys to go to the beach and head to the Cove at the south end. We'd set up and take turns watching the surfers, taking a walk, and sleeping. It's the best view in south Jersey. We'd spend the morning there and then go to the Acme, where we'd buy everything we'd need for a barbecue lunch. While there, we'd make reservations for dinner at the Mansion House for a half-hour after sunset. We'd call from the Acme because we won't be near a phone the rest of the day. After that, we'd go to the lighthouse. They have pavilions set up with picnic tables and barbecue grills that anyone can use. After a barbecue we'd climb the lighthouse then we'd head over to Sunset Beach in front of the concrete ship and go looking for Cape May Diamonds. From there we'd walk north to Higbees beach. Then we'd head back to Sunset Beach for the flag-lowering ceremony and to watch the dolphins. Later, we'd go to the Mansion House with a bottle of Gallo Café Zinfandel Red because it's BYO. It's a gourmet seafood restaurant but it also has the best steak in town. From there we'd cruise through the mall and go to Cabanas, check out some music and have a couple more drinks. If it was a hot night, we'd drive to Cape May Point to an undisclosed site and skinny-dip.

a little bit of cotton wool gets in the way. Now are you going to let a little bit of cotton wool ruin your day? No. Instead, you're going to fill your day with culture and shopping. Besides, you don't have much choice, not like the old days, when people would come to the Shore and at the first sight of rain, would get in their cars and go home, leaving the poor hotel twisting in the wind (and rain). Credit card deposits changed all that (incidentally, the first credit card ever issued was a Diners Club card in 1951).

So anyway, after breakfast, get in the car and drive down Washington Street, to the **Emlen Physick Estate** and enjoy a tour through a house that symbolizes the rebirth of Cape May. It was this enchanting structure that caused a political battle in the early 1970s when a group of preservationists fought a hopelessly shortsighted city council that was happy to see the place fall down. Within a few years, the mansion was saved and the preservationists took over the council, the Mid-Atlantic Center for the Arts was set up and took over the house, and Cape May was on its way back as the town realized its lifeblood was its amazing Victorian heritage. Spend the best part of an hour poring over the details of this beautifully-restored house. Even if this isn't typically your bag, you'll feel good about yourself later if you force yourself to do it.

Next, you're going to visit the Emlen Physick store and look for some nice prints to take home and frame. Then drive back into town, park the car and head for a little shopping trip around the arts and crafts shops. Your first stop will be the **Museum Shop** at Congress Hall, which sells a quirky mixture of stuff both Cape May and otherwise. Also take a look at **Environs**, a superb

Bring a lil' hula home at the new Wanderlust store

bath and home store. There are two other stores worth visiting in Congress Hall - **Victorious**, which has a wicked collection of estate jewelry and accessories, and **39 Degrees**, one of the few Lily Pulitzer outlets in the area. After that, cross Perry Street and check out Carpenter's Square Mall, which houses gift shops like **Trading Company No. 5** and **Weather Or Knot** and browse the two galleries in here - **Art Decor** and **Tides of Time**. We also recommend you buy a specialty coffee from **MagicBrain CyberCafe** - very, very tasty.

After that, come out of the mall on Perry Street and go into the Washington Street Mall. On your right at the beginning is **Whale's Tale**, which is a browser's dream come true, with all sorts of things - jewelry, specimen shells, bath lines and classy paper goods. Across from that is **Madame's Port**, which has the coolest range of imported furniture, home decor and gifts in town. Also worth a browse is **Carli's Country Connection**, which is packed with lovely stuff for the home.

Then head for Carpenter's Lane and Jackson Street, home of **Good Scents**, which has fragrance products, candles and incense oils, jewelry, inspirational books and tons of other lovely things. Cross Jackson and check out the building that houses **Bath Time**, **Guardian** and **Mariah's**. The next stop on this shopping crawl is the wonderfully-quirky gift store **Trade Winds** on Lafayette Street.

At this stage, you'll be ready for a hearty lunch. There are several good options around the shopping area. You can get fine soups, sandwiches and lunch specials from the following places: **The Ugly Mug** and **The Pilot House** (next door to each other on Washington Street Mall), **Jackson Mountain Cafe** (on Jackson Street), **The Blue Pig** at Congress Hall, and **Depot Market Cafe** (Elmira Street, just off Lafayette).

After that, continue your epic shop with a visit to **Wanderlust** on Jefferson (next to the Cape May Day Spa). Wanderlust has a mouthwatering selection of cool furniture and gifts with a strong coastal theme. This place is a blast. Then you're going to make the short trip to West Cape May. Stop at **Up In Smoke**, a new upscale men's gift gallery and cigar store, a welcome addition to the female-biased stores in town. Then go around the corner to Park Boulevard and spend some time going through the eclectic bunch of stores in town. The first section of Park contains **The Flying Fish Studio**, official T-shirt suppliers to *Exit Zero*. After that, drive to the next part of Park, where you'll find **Kate's**

MY PERFECT DAY
Karin Rickard, GM, Martini Beach

I'LL GET up early around 7:30, or 8, take an outside shower and make myself some freshly squeezed orange and grapefruit juice. Then, I'll take my pups, Ellie and Jackson, down to the Higbee's Beach parking lot. I'll take the road off to the right and drive all the way down to the canal area, then I'll go out on the beach and run the dogs until they can't run anymore and then drive back home. Then, I'll try to get out on a boat and fish with anyone that'll have me. The best part of the day is going out fishing, catching dinner, and then getting back and docking. It's the greatest, just being part of that team out there. I stay out until they tell me I have to come in. When my friends and I get back, we clean the boat and somebody guts the fish. I take the filets back to my house, pick up a couple of cases of beer at Collier's Liquor Store on the way home. After I get home and put the fish on ice and the beer in the fridge, I take another shower and run over to Tradewinds and see what Lissie has got in as far as jewelry goes and dump a hundred bucks on myself. That's probably my favorite thing to do here, shopping at Tradewinds when Lissie's there. She owns the shop and she's got the coolest, most affordable stuff. When she's there you're in a fantasyland, like a party in itself. She lets you try on everything. It's the funnest shopping ever. Then I go back home, everyone comes over and I have a big fish fry with all my friends. Then we chill and look at the beautiful sky. The sky here is just amazing.

A trolley tour through the Historic District is a must. *Photo by MAC*

Flowers, **A Place on Earth** (the best soap shop for miles and miles around), the **Spiral Gift Shop** and **Vintage Cottage,** both of which provide pleasurable browsing experiences.

After that, you're ready for a trolley ride through the Historic District. We realize a rainy day isn't the perfect scenario for this but you shouldn't leave town without seeing, and hearing about, Cape May's treasures, and you're not going to walk around the streets in the rain, are you? Call the Mid-Atlantic Center for details (884-5404).

After that, you're in for a little bit of spoiling. Since you'll have checked the weather forecast in advance, you'll have made an appointment for around 4pm at the **Cape May Day Spa** on Jefferson Street or at Congress Hall. Remember that old maxim that the couple that gets massages together stays together, which is why you should book the Victorian Experience. This is

MY PERFECT DAY
Luciano Corea, City Administrator

I'D AWAKE about 8 a.m. to the sound of birds singing, a cloudless, deep blue sky, and bright sunshine streaming through my two bedroom windows. Put on a pair of shorts and a t-shirt, let the dog out and pick up the paper. Then I'd sit on the front porch with my wife Paula, drinking a cup of Twinings Breakfast Tea with the sun on my face as it warms the morning air. I'd prepare a French toast and bacon breakfast and eat on the sun porch while reading the Atlantic City Press and watching the birds fly to and from their feeder. After breakfast, I'd feed the fish in the pond and walk around the yard enjoying the plants and flowers. Then I'd pack a cooler with snacks and drinks and head for the beach with my family. Spend the afternoon at either the Cove or Poverty beach, reading my Downeast Maine magazine and walking along the shoreline with a cooling breeze blowing, heading toward the lighthouse if I'm at the Cove or the Coast Guard base if I go to Poverty. After my walk, probably between 4 o'clock and 5, I'll come home, clean up, and take our Cairn terrier, Slappy, for a walk through the surrounding neighborhoods. Then I'd fire up the grill and make a nice steak, with grilled asparagus and mushrooms, along with a baked potato and corn on the cob. Put on a relaxing CD and have dinner on my sun porch, watching the sunset while enjoying a nice glass of shiraz or merlot or a Guinness draft beer. After dinner, I'd take a walk through the City's historic district and the Mall, finishing with a stroll along the promenade. After my walk, I'd return home, get into bed and look forward to another "Perfect Day."

a 90-minute session which is administered by candlelight in the couple's room. Includes a soak in an oversized whirlpool tub and a side-by-side full body massage.

By now it'll be around 6pm. Go back to your room and look through your copy of *Exit Zero* newspaper and check the movie listings for the **Beach Theater**, charmingly situated a stone's throw from the ocean. It's not the flashiest movie theater, and the seats are lumpy and not so comfortable, BUT what's better than emerging from a warm and fuzzy chick-flick and being greeted by the sight of the moon over the ocean? If nothing tickles your fancy, look over the listings for **Bayshore 8**, a multiplex in North Cape May. In any event, make a plan to watch a 7.15 or 7.30pm show. This gives you time for a leisurely bath and maybe a cheeky little cocktail in your room. After you leave the movie theater, around 9:15pm, you'll be hungry (unless you stuffed your face with popcorn) and this is when you'll head for dinner at **Martini Beach**, which has wonderful tapas-style snacks – perfect for a later, lighter snack – and a chilled-out lounge.

Perfect Day for a Family #1

"There is no such thing as "fun for the whole family, " said Jerry Seinfeld. Well, we'd like to think differently. Start off with breakfast at **McGlade's**, which is situated right on the beach, near Convention Hall. The prices are decent for Cape May and the omelettes are superb.

At 10am, pile everyone in the car and get on the Garden State Parkway and take Exit 11 for the **Cape May County Zoo**. You might find it hard to believe that Cape May has an excel-

MY PERFECT DAY
Sue Lotozo, owner Flying Fish Studio

I LIKE to get up early, around six and see the sun come up over the barn next door. I have my coffee already made, because I have a timer. Usually, I am immersed in some kind of novel and I sit out on my deck if it's warm enough, have coffee and an English muffin with really tasty jam from Duckie's Market and read while my family is still sleeping. Around 7 or 7:30, I like to go down and check the waves at the Cove beach. There is a regular crowd who check the waves in the morning. You've got contractors, county workers, lawyers, you don't even know what anyone else does really. If it looks like there is anything going on, I'll go back home, get the surfboards and wake up my oldest daughter Eliza and go surfing before work. If there aren't any waves, I bring my skates and skate from the Cove to just before Convention Hall on the promenade. I'll get off and go up Gurney Street make a right, go past the Chalfonte, past the water tower and end up back at the Cove. After that I go to work between 10 and 3 then I'll go home and make a picnic basket with fresh veggies, peanut butter and jelly, leftovers, and juices. I get my kids and take them to the Cove. Other people in town who work day jobs are also just arriving, so we know a lot of them. The best thing in the world is when there is a beautiful sunset and there are waves and I'm with my kids and my husband Joe. Sometimes there are potluck dinners. We'll bring a salad, and someone else will bring lasagna. There's a guy that brings a crock pot and plugs it into the pavilion outlet and makes meatballs then we have meatball sandwiches. We share a lot. It's like a ritual.

A superb zoo is only a 20-minute drive from town. *Photo: Maciej Nabrdalik*

lent zoo. Most likely, you'll be surprised it has one at all. Well it does, and it IS excellent. Every year, more than 300,000 people turn up to see the 170 species of animals, including lions, tigers, giraffes, camels and Marlboro lights, in 128 beautiful wooded acres. There's also a children's playground, where your kids can roam freely and fool around with the lions, cougars and grizzly bears – don't worry, grizzlies LOVE to wrestle with toddlers. The zoo is open from 10am-4.45pm, seven days a week, 364 days of the year. Admission is technically free but there's a donation box that we encourage you to patronize generously.

Two hours should do it for the zoo. Now drive back down the Parkway to Exit 4B, the Wildwoods. Head for the famous board-walk and enjoy a classic American day at the seaside. **Morey's Piers** have a triple treat which will keep your kids (and you, too,

MY PERFECT DAY

Connie Mahon, Municipal Clerk, Cape May Point

MY PERFECT day in Cape May begins alone at 7 a.m. with a morning jog in Cape May Point State Park followed a by a long leisurely walk along the beach to catch a few dolphins playing in the waves. After, I'd go home, water my flowers and play with my dog. Then I'd take a nice hot shower, jump into my convertible and it's off to George's Place around 10 a.m. with my husband Mike and daughter Taylor. I'd have some French toast, a great cup of coffee and good conversation with John, Aleka, Karen and George. I'd read my copy of Exit Zero over breakfast. After eating we're off to the beach. It's 85º and the sun is blazing on St. Pete's Beach in Cape May Point. All of the regulars are there saying "hi" and smiling as they pass by. My entire family is with us- Mom, Dad, Tom, Debbie and Jessica. Lifeguards Pete and Mark are on duty, guarding the beach and making their usual wise cracks. The Schuster's, all 6 of them, are sitting next to us and enjoying our "open cooler" policy, if it's in the cooler it's fair game. Art Joblin, my former Dean of Students at Drexel, is there with his usual "joke of the day" and a couple of old stories from college. The kids are all busy surfing, boogie boarding, swimming and building sand castles. Around 3 p.m. it's naptime, then a quick dip in the water and some fun with the kids. Then I'd get a little surfing in and finally be able to stand up. Mike, Taylor and I would go home around 6 p.m. to shower. After relaxing, we'd head to the Whaler's Cove (now Harpoon Henry's) to catch the sunset and have a bucket of Coronas. After a long day in the sun we'd head home and spend more quality time together. It's simple but perfect.

The bored child scenario is not one you will encounter at Morey's Piers

actually) occupied for the day. There are two waterparks and a huge amusement pier, and an endless amount of fun on tap. Altogether, Morey's has more than 100 rides and attractions, including seven world-class roller-coasters, a 160-foot high ferris wheel and more than 30 kiddie rides. For lunch, there are about a million options on the boardwalk, and we're not even going to begin to make a recommendation, apart from saying that Curley's fries has a really, really cool big sign (of, wait for it, a curly fry).

MY PERFECT DAY
Bob Jackson, mayor of West Cape May

I'D GET up around 4:30 a.m., take my fishing rod and walk on the South Cape May beach toward Cape May Point. When I find a good spot, I'd cast metal or a swimming lure and fish until just after daybreak. After fishing, I'd meander around, look for seashells and do some bird watching. I enjoy the serenity and quiet of being alone with the walkers and joggers. Then I'd keep walking all around Cape May Point and continue toward Higbee's Beach. If you look toward the bay this early in the morning, you'll see porpoise starting to play, actively feeding, and doing cartwheels in the water. After my walk, I'd go and get an espresso somewhere and then have an egg and pork roll sandwich at Bella Vida Garden Café on Broadway. After breakfast, I'd take a bike ride around the entire island for a real hard workout. Then I'd relax, either working in my surf fishing shop or doing things around the house with friends and family. About an hour before sunset, I'd go fishing again, but this time I'd start on Sunset Beach. Here you can see the porpoise coming back in the opposite direction, the sun dipping in the ocean and the flag lowering for the nightly ceremony. You can't beat it.

By the way, if you're a big ninny when it comes to riding rollercoasters and such like, Morey's have three classes of rides, from Mild Thrill to High Thrill Attractions.

You should be about done by 6pm. Back to your rooms for a shower and a change into nice clothing (think cool cotton whites and blacks for that Mediterranean feel). At around 7pm or so you'll be ready for a beautiful family portrait that will be an oh-so poignant reminder of the great day you just all had together. Call **MP Myers Photography**, who specializes in this kind of thing. Mary Pat likes to shoot in natural light, just before sunset (884-6354).

At 8.30pm, head for a family dinner at **Henry's on the Beach**, which is a stone's throw from McGlade's, where you had breakfast this morning (assuming you're carefully following this itinerary). Henry's has a huge menu – your kids will love it. If you want to settle your nerves after your day at the theme parks, bring yourself a nice bottle of wine along – Henry's is BYO.

Now, that was easy, wasn't it?

Perfect Day for a Family #2

YOU guys better have your sea legs on today – you're going to be on the water for a good portion of the day.

Start with breakfast at **Dock Mike's**, over at the harbor, at around 8.30am. After that, continue over the Cape May bridge as if you're going to the Parkway, but instead of getting on the highway, take the right lane just over the bridge that's signposted for Ocean Drive and Wildwood. You're going to **Aqua Trails**, who you will have called a day or two previously to book a kayak trip

MY PERFECT DAY
Mark Kulkowitz, owner of the Mad Batter

MY PERFECT day would start by having breakfast at the Mad Batter around 8:30 a.m. with my friends from Philadelphia, Barb and Brian, and my wife, Pam. I'd order the Chesapeake Bay Benedict or I'd have the Eggs Croustade with a mimosa. Then I'd go golfing at the Wildwood Country Club for 18 holes because I'm a member there and that's where a lot of local people I know go. I always play 18. I'm not a beach person. My friends Barb and Brian go to the beach, they love the beach. After golfing, I'd come back, meet up with my friends when they're done with the beach and have a couple of frozen margaritas with Cuervo at a watering hole to be decided – either at Martini Beach or the Rusty Nail. Then we'd all go out to dinner at Kuishimbo's in Stone Harbor because Danny is a golfing buddy and a friend, we love Japanese food, and I like getting out of town. Or Claude's in North Wildwood. Claude used to be a chef of ours. Then if I had enough energy, I'd go see how the Mad Batter bar is doing. It's true, it's true.

for the family (884-5600) at 9.30am. They have doubles as well as single kayaks. Guide Jeff Martin, whose day job is teaching biology at Lower Cape May Regional, is a charming, chilled-out guy who'll drop in all sorts of interesting info about the trip through the beautiful wetlands that you're about to take.

After your kayak trip, it's time to give your arms a little rest and exercise those calves instead. On the bikes you'll have called up to rent the day before (see Bike Rentals in the A-Z), go on the ride to the lighthouse that's detailed on pages 26-30.

After that refreshing trip you'll now head back to the harbor to have a fun outdoor lunch on the docks at the **Lobster House Raw Bar**. You'll almost certainly have to wait for one of the tables out on the dock, but it's worth it.

After that, get back in the car and drive to New England Road, which we rather helpfully left out of our map. However, if you take Broadway north you'll see a sign for Higbees Beach to the left, just before the big bridge. Take that turn and drive for

Bay Springs Farm is a must-visit to see the cute, peace-loving, seriously-curious alpacas.
Photo: Zoey Sless-Kitain

MY PERFECT DAY
Jerry Inderwies, Cape May fire chief

I'D HEAD to the Texas Avenue Wawa for my 20-ounce coffee at around 6:30 a.m. Then I'd go to the OV for breakfast, the Ocean View on Broadway and Grant, for the #4 scrambled. Then I'd come home, get ready for the beach, get my three daughters dressed for the beach about noonish and go to the beach on Philadelphia Avenue until about four. I grew up on that beach, been there my whole life, was in the beach patrol from 1986 to 88. Then I'd head home and have a Coors Light on my back deck, get a babysitter for the kids and go to Cucina Rosa for dinner, my wife and I. Then we'd end the night at the Ugly Mug and head home about midnight, depending on whether we had a good babysitter.

Tom Carroll, owner Mainstay Inn
OUR first most favorite thing in the morning is having coffee on our own porch. After, we'd do a bird walk with the Cape May Bird Observatory, especially if Pete Dunne leads it. We love the light lunch at the Twinings Tearoom, looking over the grounds and gardens on the patio behind the carriage house. After, we'd take a tandem bike ride to the northern side of town and back. Around 5:30 p.m. just as everybody's leaving, including the lifeguards and beach tag inspectors, we'd take a walk on the beach below Convention Hall. It's the best time for a walk or a swim. The sun is lower in the sky and a nice breeze is over the ocean. There are a lot of serious Cape May beachgoers who wait until that time to go.

PERFECT DAYS

a mile or two until you see a sign for **Bay Springs Alpaca Farm** on your left. Alpacas are like cuddly little camels and they can be pretty sociable, too, especially Chanel, who might even come up and smack you on the lips. Visit the great little store at the back of the house – there are lots of touchy-feely alpaca goods to entice you. The farm is open to visitors Friday to Sunday (you can call Barbara or Warren ahead of time on 884-0563).

Now you're ready for your third trip to the harbor (okay, so it's not the most ergonomic of itineraries) for a spot of whale and dolping watching. You have two places to choose from and their names are very similar, so you can be forgiven for being confused (we've made the same mistake in the past). The first one is **Cape May Whale Watch and Research Center** (888-531-0055, www.capemaywhalewatch.com). Among other things, they run a Sunset Dolphin Watch Dinner Cruise, which starts at 6pm. The second is the **Cape May Whale Watcher** (800-786-5445, www.capemaywhalewatcher.com). They also have a Dinner Cruise, which starts at 6.30pm. We're going to let you make the choice of sunset cruises if that's okay with you.

Perfect Rainy Day for a Family

Keeping the kids amused on a rainy day in Cape May... that has to be a monster challenge, right? Actually, we think you might just pull it off with this little itinerary. Either that, or just hire a really good babysitter for the whole day and night, dump the little brats and go off for a Perfect Rainy Day for a Couple (see page 79).

Let's begin this day with a 9am breakfast at **McDonald's**. It's only a five minute drive from town, and it's one of the friendliest,

MY PERFECT DAY
Hanna Miller, Cape May local

I'M 17 years old and I was born and raised in Cape May. I now live in New York City but I still return here every summer to visit friends and work in my parents' two restauraunts, 410 Bank Street and Frescos. My day starts with breakfast at Uncle Bill's or George's Place, two pancake houses on the beach. Then I'll grab my surfboard and headphones and bike to the Cove, the most serene section of the two-mile-long shore. While waiting for the surf to come up I might walk or jog along the coastline toward the lighthouse. Rounding Cape May point you reach the WWII concrete bunker that used to nestle in the sand until the ocean eroded the beach, leaving this hulking barrack hovering 10 feet in the air supported by thin, stilt-like supports. Over here you may see pods of dolphins jumping just off the shore. Upon returning to my surfboard I'll attempt to catch a few waves and then bike home around 5pm (late in the day the beach is less crowded and the sun is softer). Then I'll grab dinner at Gecko's at Carpenter Square Mall. Ask for Jill, she's a fabulous waitress. After dinner, a walk around the mall and a little shopping. Visit the Free Shop a very hip women's clothing store (with better clothes than many boutiques back home in New York). Around 10pm, I head up to the boardwalk to catch a late movie at the Beach Theater across the street, or relive my childhood playing in the arcade or hitting a round of mini golf. See you at the shore!

A Coast Guard helicopter at the NAS Aviation Museum

best-run Mickey Ds that you'll experience. It even has a built-in fireplace for extra coziness. You'll find it at Bayshore Road and Sandman, a mile or so before you get to the ferry.

After that, you're going take them to the **Naval Air Station Wildwood Aviation Museum**, which is run by a real local hero, Dr. Joseph Salvatore. The museum is at Cape May County Airport in Rio Grande, around a 15-minute drive from town. The station served as a training facility for dive-bomber squadrons throughout World War Two and, at its peak, accommodated 222 planes and nearly 17,000 takeoffs and landings per month. Thirty-eight airmen died while training at the site. Now the base is a museum, lovingly cared for by Dr. Salvatore, with a fascinating collection of planes and helicopters. Call (609) 886-8787 for more information and visit www.usnasw.org.

The country store at beautiful Cold Spring Village

Next is a short drive to **3J's Wildwood Bowl**, at 3401 New Jersey Avenue. It has 32 lanes and is the nearest bowling hall to Cape May. After 90 minutes of bowling, it'll be around 12.30pm and you're going to take a leisurely drive back into Cape May, all the way down Beach Avenue until you see the big Atlas Inn on your left. Park here and make your way into **Yesterday's Heroes Ballpark Cafe**, which has a fantastic collection of baseball memorabilia and a mechanical pony ride that children can ride for free. The menu is diverse and fun, and includes a Little League menu for children.

Be sure to finish lunch before 2pm, because that's when you're going to be catching one of the beautiful old trains that are run by **Cape May Seashore Lines** that leaves from Lafayette Street (www.cmsllr.com for more information). Take the 15-minute trip to **Cold Spring Village** (www.hcsv.org), a 19th century open-air living history museum. The village has loads of cool demonstrations in 25 restored historic buildings on a 22-acre wood-

Don't miss a trip with Cape May Seashore Lines. *Photo: David Gray*

ed site where costumed interpreters bring the crafts, sights, sounds, and aroma of the Age of Homespun to life. You can catch the old train back to Cape May at 3.30pm.

For that evening, you're going to make reservations for the family at **Elaine's Dinner Theater**, which puts on good quality fun shows that resemble pantomime. The food and the theater is geared toward the family, and they're actually laugh-out-loud funny. Elaine's was voted one of the Top Five Dinner Theaters in the country by the Food Network. For more information and reservations, call (609) 884-4358.

We thought about recommending bedtime reading for your children, but you can take responsibility for that.

A Great Old Time

In town for a short visit and needing some quality retail therapy? Join *Stefanie Godfrey* on an antique crawl.

CAPE May and the surrounding areas are full of specialty antique stores just waiting for you to come in and explore. Here's a guide to some of the best. When you pull into town over the bridge, you'll see some landmarks that give Cape May its character. The boats in the marinas, the Lobster House, and **WS Antiques** are just a few. Since WS is on the right as you drive past, let's make this our first stop. WS has its own parking lot, which you will come to appreciate later in your trip. Check out the items on display outside of the store. There are old tubs, birdbaths, old window shutters and radiators. The open-air selling adds a bit of fresh-ness and casualness to what could be a stuffy experience.

Inside is a mouthwatering array of all sorts of stuff that owner Bill Saponaro gets from more than 120 antique and col-lectible dealers. So in addition to beautiful antiques, you'll also come across some yard sale finds. Just a sampling of items you'll find are hats, dishes, teapots, kids' toys, cool old postcards and, of course, plenty of antique furniture. When you've gotten your fill, mosey out to your car, hop in and pull out carefully because people tend to come over the bridge going very fast.

Now it's time to go further into town. Go straight down Lafayette until you see the only stop sign at the dead end in front of Collier's liquor store. Turn left at the stop sign and then make an immediate right. Keep your eyes peeled for an available metered parking spot and make the next left on to Perry. Take in the awesome view of the Atlantic and the big yellow house by the sea, Congress Hall. There is parking along Perry and along the smaller roads surrounding the hotel. If you've exhausted your mind and nerves trying to find a space, which can prove to be tricky in season, then pull in front of Congress Hall and have a valet do the work for you – after all, you've got shopping to do.

As you enter the famous hotel, through its breezeway and two sets of heavy double doors, you'll see a long corridor of shops on the right. Walk down the aisle and head in to **Victorious**. Apart from selling fine gifts and antiques this nicely adorned shop specializes in mostly estate jewelry, according to manager and gemologist, Jennifer Papendick Tozer. Victorious not only carries estate jewelry but also specializes in antique jewelry appraisal. Even if you aren't purchasing, it's fun just to try on some of the antique diamonds. The shop's chi could perhaps be summed up by the sign hung on the wall behind the counter that reads, "Your husband called, he said to buy anything you want" and, oh, you WILL want to spend some coin on the gorgeous chandeliers, mirrors and furniture.

Next, head for 668 Washington Street, the **Ellen Christine Millinery**. Owner Ellen Christine's main shop is in Chelsea, New York, but she also operates this outlet store here on the island. Vintage fashion enthusiasts beware. You may not leave this place for a long time. There are so many articles of clothing to try on, look at, and be mesmerized by. The vintage collars and animal wraps (with heads still intact) are just two of the unique items this store offers. There are also, purses, shoes, belts, and completely decadent feather boas.

If you keep walking up Washington, you'll come across **Olde Lights/Finishing Touches of Cape May**. There are lamps of all shapes and sizes filling up the small, cozy store. What is so fancy about old lamps, you ask? Well, for one thing, the lamps sold here are made to last and to be repaired when they break, instead of just thrown away. Owner Bob Anderson just happens to do repairs in the back of his store. Try not to drool over the exquisite pieces you'll find here, like the pink, beaded lamp with black trim from the 1950s. There are varieties of kerosene, gas and electric lamps and they're mostly all redone with vintage fabrics.

Now it's on to the corner of West Perry and Myrtle, where you'll find the tiny **Out of the Past Antiques**. When you walk in you'll instantly see why owner Jeanne Hermann says for her "it's all about memories." There are vintage postcards, old photos and trade cards, which were small business card types made by manufacturers for stores, who put their name on them and handed them out to prospective buyers. There are such neat and inexpensive items you could spend a long time here, buy lots of stuff, and not wear out your wallet. Jeanne, a retired librarian, hands out a free book to every child that comes in her store. Hardback classics like *Emmit Otter's Jug Band Christmas* lie in a basket just waiting for takers.

When you get back on Perry, make your next right on to Park

Blvd in West Cape May. Follow it until you come to **The Antique Doorknob**. It's "the oldest antique shop in Cape May," according to owner Bill Causey. "We get the name for a reason," says Bill. His shop is filled with all different types of doorknobs, glass and metal. The most expensive ones cost $10,000 for a set of five, but don't let that scare you – they come in all price ranges. In addition, they offer a nice selection of fireplace mantels, lights, and chandeliers.

We'll finish up with our final stop at **Sheen Falls** on the corner of Pearl and Broadway. As you pull your car out of the lot make a left back onto Park, go up to Pearl Ave and make a right. Follow Pearl to Broadway. As you get close, find a place to park along the street. There are no meters here and usually plenty of parking on the side streets. Sheen Falls was opened last May by Colm O'Brien. Colm's been in the business for five years and his selection includes antiques and distinct treasures from all corners of the globe. Some of the more memorable items include beautiful oriental vases, pretty French statues, and exotic bowls handmade by South African artisans living in the Western Cape.

If you've worked up an appetite, get back into your car and head down Broadway until you reach the light at Sunset. Turn right and then quickly left into **Vanthia's** restaurant, where you can sit, have coffee and a delicious pastry or eat a full meal with yummy options like Spinach Quiche and Greek salad or their delicious Crab Cake sandwich. The service is friendly and warm and the décor reflects that vibe. When you've been given the check and stretched your legs as you stand up from your meal, you can give a kiss to your mate on a job well done.

A Charmed Town

Cape May shopkeeper Gus Correia explains why we're so lucky to live (and vacation) here

IF you're lucky enough to be in Cape May, you're lucky enough. What a special place. If this is your first visit, you're in for a treat (especially if you follow the advice in this book) and if you're a Cape May addict, well you already know you are. As a shop owner, I'm often asked, "What's a good place to eat." And the answer? "Where d'you want to begin?" There are more five-star eateries here than any small town has a right to. Take a stroll around town and pore over the menus posted outside, though, here's a tip: reserve, reserve and reserve.

Naturally, quality doesn't always come cheap, and prices can get high around here. If you're a family on a fixed budget, check out the early bird specials. Last summer, I enjoyed prime rib, all the fixings, no crowds and great service for $10. And there were a couple cold beers and a tip involved, too.

If you feel like cooking your own little treat, you've got some amazing fresh seafood to choose from and when we say fresh here, we mean fresh. You can watch the stuff being unloaded every day from the boats at the Lobster House. Here's a tip: Hit the Lobster House's fish market early in the morning. By 4pm, it's

Gus and Bud

a mob scene. Steamed crabs are my thing. Buy 'em live, cook 'em yourself. You'll need some fixings and here again, Jersey fresh really is that – the corn and tomatoes are superb. It's a well-known fact to us locals that the LeGates on Bayshore Road in North Cape May has the best produce in town.

Another special thing about Cape May is that you can watch the sun rise and set over the ocean, AND watch a big ole moon rise out of the Atlantic.

Being a resort town, things do change around here, but most shops have maps and don't forget to check out the Welcome Center in the Washington Street Mall. Go there and grab as many brochures and leaflets as you can. And read 'em, too! I'm proud to be the owner of Village Leathersmith, one of the new shops that have relocated on Beach in recent years. So, in addition to the mall, you third-degree, black-belt shoppers can now shop the shore with an ocean view and breeze. What's better than that?

Eat, shop, sunbathe, swim – these are the fundamentals of any resort vacation but don't forget that Cape May has more than that. Whether on foot or by bike, you must also take some time to view the beautiful Victorian homes and gardens, whether on your own or on an organized tour.

From the beachfront, have a great Cape May day!

JOS H HAND

CHAPTER FOUR
Out Of Season

Come on Down!

So it isn't summer – so what. It doesn't have to be hot for Cape May to be cool.

CAN you imagine being a hotelier or restaurant owner in Cape May in, say, the 30s, or even 70s – in fact, any decade you care to name up until the late 80s? Back in the day, it was a six-week season and you simply prayed for sun and hoped for the best. The Cape May of today is a very different proposition, though, thanks to the inventiveness and determination of the Mid-Atlantic Center for the Arts (MAC), and a group of resourceful hotel and B&B owners who wouldn't give up on this town.

Now you can come to Cape May for 12 months of the year and still come home with good memories. Okay, make that 11 or more likely 10, because we're not even going to try and sell you on January (and we're only going to use the March listing as an excuse to crack a joke, as you'll read in a moment or two). On the other hand, there's a very strong argument for coming down here and having a snuggly weekend at a great hotel, for a fraction of the price you'd pay in summer.

So here is our three-season guide to enjoying America's original resort town.

FEBRUARY This is when Cape May briefly awakes from

Snow on the water – a weirdly beautiful sight. *Photo: Jeanie Schiff*

the January slumber – and then goes right back to sleep again. **St. Valentine's** weekend always surprises the locals with how busy the town suddenly becomes for two nights. There are nice little touches, like the light show put on by Congress Hall, which has become the Empire State building of Cape May – during St. Valentine's weekend, the majestic old hotel is bathed in pink. If you do plan to spend a romantic weekend in this most romantic of towns, just make sure you book your room AND your restaurant choice ahead of time. Give yourself a month for the room and at least a week's notice for the restaurant, otherwise you'll be sharing a giant hoagie from WaWa on February the 14th.

MARCH If you like watching men doing construction work, then this is the month for you to visit because that's pretty much all that goes on here. If you like the idea of birding but are too afraid to ask, then the good folks at the **Cape May Bird**

Keisa Brown rocks Cabanas during the Jazz Festival in April

Observatory normally run a Birding for First-Timers weekend at the end of March. Call them on (609) 884-2736 for details.

APRIL The nationally-respected **Cape May Jazz Festival** happens in the middle of the month. It's one of two jazz festivals (the other is in November) and it's a barnstorming weekend of entertainment if you're a jazz fan – the town really comes alive, which is a great boon for the restaurant, hotel and bar owners. There's the **Spring Festival**, organized by MAC, which normally runs from the end of April to the beginning of May. If you're a keen gardener, or want to be, this is definitely worth a weekend trip. There are lectures and workshops, demonstrations and shows. Check out MAC's website for more details – www.capemaymac.org.

MAY This is when the **Cape May Music Festival**, also organized by MAC, begins. The festival was launched in 1989 and has grown into a strong event with as wide a variety as you could possibly wish for – from classical to folk, Irish to opera, Flamenco to Doo Wop. Again, check out MAC's website or call them on 800-275-4278. Another event worth coming down for in May is **Crafts & Antiques at Memorial Day,** when the Convention Hall fills up with more than 40 regional craftsmen and artisans offering a wide selection of crafts, folk art, custom jewelry and more.

SEPTEMBER First of all, September is a great month to visit Cape May. Accommodation is cheaper, the restaurants are a little quieter (if that appeals to you), and the weather is still gorgeous. In terms of events, there is the **Food & Wine Festival**, which usually runs for the third week of the month. It's a lot of fun with lectures, hands-on workshops, tastings and luncheons. Learn as you sam-

Who says Cape May doesn't have range? Left, celebrating Victorian Week; right, Billy Baldwin followed Susan Sarandon as guest of honor at the Cape May NJ State Film Festival. *Photos: Jenn Heinold, Lulu Laidlaw-Smith*

ple the best that the restaurant capital of New Jersey has to offer. There are five nights of chefs' dine-arounds, Gourmet Tasting and Restaurant Tour, The People's Choice Chowder Contest and the Festival Lobster Bake. If you're an enthusiastic gourmand, MAC offer a Full Package, which includes admission to all the major events, three days of classes, tastings, seminars and a limited edition cookbook. Visit www.capemaymac.org for more details.

OCTOBER The highlight of this busy month is **Victorian Week**. Rated one of North America's Top 100 Events, this is a 10-day celebration featuring historic house tours, Victorian fashion shows, murder mystery dinners, vintage dance workshop, brass band concerts, crafts and antique shows. Visit www.capemaymac.org for details. At the beginning of the month is the day-long **Oktoberfest**, when beautiful Jackson Street gets taken over by overweight men wearing lederhosen and eating fat sausages. The **Lima Bean Festival** in West Cape May is usually a lot more fun – it happens in the middle of October. Halloween is a great time to be in Cape May and we strongly recommend **Congress Hall's Phantom Ball**, held in the magnificent ballroom. The hotel offers packages for the event as well as individual tickets (www.congresshall.com).

NOVEMBER The second **Jazz Festival** of the year happens the second week, and it's followed by the fast-emerging **Cape May New Jersey State Film Festival**, which only launched in 2001 and which has attracted stars like Susan Sarandon and Billy Baldwin as guests of honor. Visit www.njstatefilmfestival.com.

DECEMBER Cape May at Christmas makes you feel like a kid again. Highlights are the **Christmas Candlelight House Tours**,

Congress Hall lights up during the holiday season. *Photo: Imagic Digital*

self-guided evening tours of festively decorated homes, inns, hotels and churches; and the **Dickens Christmas Extravaganza**, which features performances, lectures and feasts to really put you in the mood for the holidays. Visit capemaymac.org to get details on both of these events. And finally there is the **West Cape May Christmas Parade**, usually the second Saturday in December, when crowds line the streets to watch an elaborate parade up Broadway and into town. Check out www.westcapemaytoday.com for more details nearer the time.

Then there's New Year's Eve, but we figure you can handle that one on your own.

CHAPTER FIVE
The Listings

THE BLUE PIG TAVERN

There is one particular time to visit the restaurant at Congress Hall – and that's any time. On beautiful sunny days the patio is a delightful spot to start your day with a breakfast of, say, The Blue Pig Skillet – two eggs, crispy potatoes, jack cheese, avocado, sour cream and spicy salsa. Or linger over lunch with a crab cake salad as you sip an iced tea and watch the people strolling to the outdoor mall and heading for the beach. The Blue Pig is also a great spot to enjoy the last light of day as the sun sets over the water, just one block away. On crisp or chilly evenings, in the spring, fall or winter, the large fireplace in the Blue Pig, decorated by Cape May Diamonds hand-picked from the beach at the Point, comes alive and turns the place into a cozy little tavern where you can enjoy classic American bistro cuisine such as homemade lasagne, old-fashioned turkey pot pie and steak frites with bearnaise sauce. *251 Beach Ave., (609) 884-8422, www.congresshall.com.*

THE BOILER ROOM

This sleek club was carved out of the basement of Congress Hall and often surprises the first-time visitor, given that its modern, industrial chic look (stone walls and metal tables, softened with dark velvet cushions and fabrics) is a visual departure from the rest of the hotel. The Boiler Room is now open seven nights a week, 9pm-3am, during the season and recently revamped its schedule. There's now live jazz five nights a week, interspersed with cool loungey music played through the hotel's sound system. This combination sits nicely with the sexy, intimate feel of the club – dozens of strategically-placed votives give the place a feel that conjures up images of speakeasies and Morocco. The Boiler Room also has a comedy night on Mondays, which is a refreshing new addition to Cape May nightlife. Another welcome bonus is a new late-night menu, from 10pm-2am, serving good, basic munchie food. *Entrance on Perry Street.*, (609) 884-6507, *www.congresshall.com.*

THE BROWN ROOM

Named simply for its chocolate-brown color scheme, Congress Hall's cocktail lounge is a favored spot in town. In summer the place exudes an elegance and style that reminds the drinker of, say, 1930s Cuba or The Great Gatsby (depending on how many Blue Pig Martinis he or she has had). In summer and on warm spring and fall evenings you can enjoy the vibe of this beautifully-designed room or walk out to the veranda and spend an hour or two on the classic Kennedy rockers, maybe staring up at the moon as it shines on the ocean or gazing at the pool lights over at the cabana – even out here, the lounge's stylish, black-clad cocktail servers will be happy to serve you. If you're in the mood for a snack, you can order from the Blue Pig Tavern's menu. On colder evenings, the room glows with the logs ablaze in the large stone fireplace – come here for after-dinner drinks in March or November and you won't want to leave. *251 Beach Ave., (609) 884-8421, www.congresshall.com.*

CABANAS

A big favorite with locals all year round, this lively beachfront bar and restaurant is a Cape May must-visit. By day, Cabanas is a terrific place to kick back and sample the Caribbean-influenced menu, which specializes in seafood. On warm days, the doors open up and the breeze from the Atlantic floats in. Cabanas is a great place to bring the family – there's a large children's menu and kids four and under eat for free. At night, the place really comes alive, with something going on in every corner. There's the brand-new Tiki Sea's Rum and Raw Bar, which has oysters, steamed and chilled shrimp, clams, mussels and fish tacos – and 22 frozen and rum martinis to choose from. You can also order from the late-night menu until 2am. Every night there's live music from DJs and bands, including the legendary Bluebone, and the large dancefloor is usually bustling. Cabanas is also Cape May's eight-ball headquarters, with two pool tables. *Beach Ave. at Decatur, (609) 884-4800, www.cabanasonthebeach.com.*

CAPE ORIENT

There are two reason why Cape Orient is a must-visit during your stay in Cape May. The first is that it's one of the best Asian restaurants in south Jersey, serving Chinese, Japanese and Thai. The second is that even though this is Oriental fine dining at its best, a main course at Cape Orient will only cost you anything from a half to a THIRD of what you'll pay at any of the town's other leading restaurants. In fact, you'll often see other restaurant owners as well as innkeepers and local dignitaries eating in here. Cape Orient is the only restaurant on the island that serves sushi and don't think that a restaurant cannot manage to do Chinese, Thai and Japanese equally well – we've tried them all here, and the same standards of excellence apply right across the board. This is no surprise given that owners Glendy and Jack Hwang have built a reputation on offering the finest Asian cuisine in the area. *Washington Commons Mall, near the Acme, (609) 898-0088, BYO, www.capeorient.com.*

CARNEY'S

"If you don't visit Carney's, you didn't come to Cape May" is what they say at this popular bar and restaurant, situated on the beachfront. There are two sides to Carney's – the Main Room and the Other Room. The Main Room is a lively place that attracts a young, sexy crowd. Some of the best party bands in the Tri-state area belt out pop favorites that pack the dancefloor, and a new hip-hop band will be playing throughout the summer of 2004. Then there are the famous regulars like karaoke night, the Sunday Jam Sessions and the Hawaiian Tropic Model Search. In the Other Room, the tone is more mellow. The entertainment in here includes local jazz legend Lois Smith, who'll be performing Thursday, Saturday and Sunday. On other nights, there will be performances by accomplished jazz musicians from New York, Baltimore and Philadelphia. Both rooms serve an extensive menu until 10pm every night. *Beach Avenue and Jackson, (609) 884-4424.*

COPPER FISH

The first thing you appreciate about this new restaurant (it opened in the summer of 2003) is the interior – it's the coolest on the island. The Italian-style white leather chairs contrast beautifully with the dark wooden floor, while the copper finishes and carvings that grace the walls add just the right touch of decoration. And the enclosed fireplace means that Copper Fish looks just as inviting in October as it does in July or August. Then there's the food, which stands up to the high standards set by the decor. Starters include smoked tuna pizza, with pico de gallo salsa and lime sour cream; and crispy calamari over napa cabbage served with sweet chili dipping sauce. The list of entrees include a superb blackened tuna; smoked tomato and jalapeno crab cakes; smoked chili filet; and black bean chicken. The location is pretty special, too – Copper Fish is located across from South Jersey Marina, right on the harbor. *1246 Rt. 109 South, (609) 898-0354, BYO.*

DANIEL'S ON BROADWAY

Cape May is famous for the quality of its restaurants, and Daniel's is as good as it gets. The Food Network recently voted it one of the top five BYO restaurants in the country, and no wonder – chef/owner Harry Gleason's creations are works of art. The chili-crusted pork loin, grilled with a paste of ancho and chipotle chili powders, Southwestern spices and honey, tastes even better than it looks in this photograph. Other acclaimed dishes include the pan-seared diver scallops, macadamia-crusted lamb and sesame-and-herb-crusted mahi-mahi. You might notice a lot of hyphens in the menu descriptions... chef Gleason needs them, such is his flair for inventive fusions, some of which he makes up on the spot. This is why the specials at Daniel's are worthy of particular consideration. And it's not just the food that's special – Daniel's has five intimate dining rooms on two floors of an historic magnolia Victorian mansion. *416 South Broadway, West Cape May, (609) 898-8770, BYO.*

THE EBBITT ROOM

From the moment you walk through the door, every moment of the Ebbitt Room experience smacks of class. It's located halfway along Jackson, a short but glorious streetscape of Victorian B&Bs, private homes and the Virginia, a boutique hotel that's home to the Ebbitt. Before you eat, enjoy an aperitif on one of the porches that surround this immaculately-restored hotel, and then make your way into the elegant, intimate and perfectly-lit dining room. You won't find the most exotic fusions at the Ebbitt Room – that's not the style here. What you *will* experience are dishes of lamb, veal, filet steak, sea bass, halibut and scallops that are exquisitely cooked and presented. And there's the best calamari dish you're likely to taste – a very, very lightly fried dish drizzled with lime-ginger aioli. Sublime. After dinner, retire to the lounge and enjoy a cocktail as you listen to pianist Steve LaManna tinkle out some classic tunes. *25 Jackson Street, (609) 884-5700, www.virginiahotel.com.*

410 BANK STREET

This exotic restaurant has become a Cape May institution, along with its chef, Henry Sing Cheng, who has been cooking up a myriad of exotic dishes since the restaurant opened in 1984. Owners Steve and Janet Miller were inspired by numerous visits to the Caribbean during their former lives as Hollywood screenwriters, producers and directors, and the influences are all around here, from the luscious plants that festoon 410 Bank to the waiting staff who waltz through the restaurant in Hawaiian shirts, tossing wisecracks as they serve. But even though the atmosphere is casual, the food is wonderful. *The New York Times* wrote that people would make the trip from Manhattan to Cape May just to eat at 410 Bank – and "it's worth it," the paper added. Among the favorites – New Orleans voodoo shrimp, yellowfin tuna with Chef Sing's famous Barbadian black bean sauce, and Atlantic swordfish with a champagne crab-meat cream sauce. *410 Bank Street, (609) 884-2127, BYO.*

FOOD & DRINK

GECKO'S

There are people in Cape May who equate the beginning of spring with the reopening of Gecko's and the opportunity to once again sit on the deck of this great little restaurant, sample the delicious sauces concocted by chef Randy Bithell, who runs the place with wife Susi, fill up a bucket of ice with Coronas or a fruity white and watch the world go by at this attractive spot, half a block from Congress Hall. Gecko's is the only place in town for southwestern cuisine, so if you want your chile fix, this is the place. Favorite dishes include the vegetable burrito (good veggie food is hard to come by in Cape May, and this is superb). Mind you, veggies might not want to hear about two other favorites here, which are known by some regulars as Bambi and Thumper. The former is venison medallions in an apple-bourbon glaze, and the latter is rabbit in a red chile vinegar sauce, binded with ground sunflower seeds and cornmeal. *Carpenter's Square Mall, (609) 898-7750, BYO.*

GEORGE'S PLACE

We've said it before and we'll say it again: the world would be a much better place if it was actually healthy to eat George's creamed chipped beef every morning. It's *that* good. However, seeing as your doctor wouldn't recommend such a daily intake, George's Place has plenty of other dishes that are equally good to your tastebuds and your arteries – the lemon chicken Greek salad is one of the big favorites. Since 1968, George's has been one of the best spots for breakfast, situated as it is on a corner of Beach Avenue, overlooking the ocean. Try the breakfast quesadilla or Norwegian smoked salmon. George's is also open for dinner from 5-9m from Memorial Day to Labor Day, serving classics like steak and shrimp and Greek-style calamari. The best way to describe this place? It's like you took a classic diner from Philly or New York and plonked it down right next to the ocean. Sounds good, doesn't it? *Beach Ave. and Perry Street, (609) 884-6088, BYO, www.georgesplacecapemay.com.*

HARPOON HENRY'S

If you're the kind of person that hates the idea of spending a day at the beach, showering, getting changed into a fresh T-shirt, cotton shorts and flip-flops then heading to a bar/restaurant where you can sit outside, under palm trees, 20 yards from the beach, gazing at the sun setting over the water as you sip a fruity cocktail or an ice-cold beer and snack on conch fritters or crab cakes, then Harpoon Henry's is not your kind of place. But if you *are* that kind of person, you'll be happy to know that local restaurant owners Ed and Teresa Henry recently took over Whaler's Cove and gave it a new name and a new menu. The only thing that hasn't changed is the wonderful ambience of this place – you could be in the Caribbean or Key West. Who knew North Cape May could be so exotic? Harpoon Henry's is a 10-minute drive from the center of town, not far from the ferry terminal. *Beach Drive and Browning Ave., North Cape May, (609) 886-5529.*

HENRY'S ON THE BEACH

Ed and Teresa Henry came to Cape May from Washington D.C. in 1993 and decided to stay and make a business out of their favorite little spot in the world. Their first restaurant was Zoe's (see page 145), and their second was Henry's On the Beach, which hangs over Cape May's main beach and offers up a big, diverse menu that will please everyone, which is why it's such a great place to take large groups of family or friends – a table for 10 is a breeze here. And although it's a million-dollar view (that's Ed and Teresa, above, at one of the much-coveted corner tables), the prices are among the most reasonable in town. Eat breakfast here and you might spot a pod of dolphins heading east. Eat dinner and you might see them heading back west again. Henry's also serves lunch, when the dolphins will be, um, somewhere between east and west. Incidentally, Harpoon Henry's (see opposite) is the couple's latest restaurant. *702 Beach Ave., (609) 884-8826, BYO.*

LOBSTER HOUSE

Not a lot of people know that Cape May is the second-biggest commercial fishing port on the eastern seaboard, and the Lobster House is a big part of that. There's a commercial fleet, a bustling fish market and the most successful restaurant in Cape May. There are a few different dining options available. The main restaurant serves a large and varied menu that's obviously crammed with the freshest seafood you can imagine, but which also offers meat and poultry dishes. And then there's the Raw Bar, with its wildly-popular tables by the docks. Sitting here with a pitcher of beer, tucking into lobster and crab as you chat and stare out over the harbor is as good as it gets. There is usually a wait for a table here in summer, but the turnaround is fast, so do hang around – it's worth it. Also make sure you take some time to enjoy a cocktail at the permanently-docked Schooner American, which also has its own menu. *Fisherman's Wharf, (609) 884-8296, www.thelobsterhouse.com.*

MAGICBRAIN CYBERCAFE

It's never been a problem finding great food in Cape May, but great coffee? A little trickier. This is why the arrival of MagicBrain CyberCafe in 2003 was a good thing. MagicBrain has fresh-ground Green Mountain coffee, which means classic coffee, espresso and lattes. But there's more – MagicBrain offers a superb variety of specialty coffees with tasty combos, like Japanese Latte (orange, almond and cherry flavors), Chunky Monkey Cappuccino (chocolate, banana and hazelnut) and lots of others. There are also specialty teas, delicious Italian sodas (try the Key Lime Cream Cooler), plus gourmet pastries, bagels and late-night desserts. AND it's about time we mentioned that MagicBrain offers high-speed internet access and 12 computers so that you can keep up to date with email and surf the net. Or bring your own computer – MagicBrain is a Wi-Fi hotspot. *31 Perry Street, (609) 884-8188 & 4807 Pacific Ave., Wildwood, 729-8550, www.magicbraincybercafe.com.*

THE MAGNOLIA ROOM AT THE CHALFONTE

The Magnolia Room restaurant is the heart of The Chalfonte Hotel, established in 1876. Chefs Dot Burton and Lucille Thompson are daughters of the late Helen Dickerson, who cooked there for 60 years. The restaurant regularly receives national acclaim, most recently on the Discovery Channel's *Home Matters*, and on *Tyler's Ultimate* on the Food Network. The fried chicken was named one of the Top Ten best in the country by *USA Today*. Breakfast features hot and cold buffet with Southern specialties, and dinner includes a choice from four entrees (including vegetarian), soup or appetizer, salad, sides and dessert. Fine wines and cocktails are also available. Before or after dinner (or both!), you should check out the King Edward Bar, or sit with your drink on one of the porch rockers and watch the horses and carriages go by. The Chalfonte features nightly entertainment with music, cabaret and theater. *301 Howard St., (609) 884-8409, www.chalfontehotel.com*.

MANSION HOUSE

In a town blessed with hundreds of Victorian masterpieces, this modest little building tucked behind Cape May's version of the big green monster – Collier's Liquor Store – doesn't stand out from the crowd. However, it houses what many consider to be Cape May's finest seafood restaurant. The executive chef is Joe Lotozo, who's been at the helm (or better yet, the stove) since the restaurant opened five years ago. Lotozo also opened another of Cape May's finest restaurants, The Ebbitt Room, in 1989. Favorite appetizers include fried calamari with an ancho chili-aioli and tomato-scallion relish; and sashimi-grade raw tuna with apples, mint, jicama and wasabi mayonnaise. Classic main courses include the wasabi and macadamia nut-encrusted salmon and the 21-day-aged black angus filet with a Jack Daniels whisky sauce. The restaurant is open from May to October. *Mansion Street, (609) 884-0200, BYO, www.mansion houseseafood.com.*

MARTINI BEACH

There are a few adjectives that could be thrown at this newly-renovated cocktail lounge and restaurant. Here are some: hippest, coolest, friendliest. And if funnest was a proper word, we'd throw that in there, too. Suffice to say that first of all Martini Beach has a to-die-for location: you can eat dinner in the glassed-in balcony that feels like it hangs out over the beach, it's that close. Then there is the cleverly-designed menu, which encourages tapas-style dining, which means that if you and your pals can't decide between the rare seared tuna, the pierogis, the salt-and-pepper calamari or the paprika-rubbed ribs, you can order them all in smaller portions and share your heart out! Martini Beach feels like the kind of place where Marilyn Monroe might have shared a sneaky martini with F. Scott Fitzgerald, Mae West and Errol Flynn (and then boogied their heart out to Outkast on the always-popular dancefloor). *Beach Ave. at Decatur, above Cabanas, (609) 884-1925.*

THE MERION INN

The Merion Inn, circa 1885, has delighted generations of Cape May locals and visitors with traditional regional seafood, sizzling steaks and classic cocktails ("the best place in Cape May to get a martini," according to *Philadelphia* magazine). Enjoy live jazz piano every evening while having a martini at the oldest bar in Cape May or feasting on stuffed lobster or prime rib in one of four candlelit Victorian dining rooms. The staff is friendly and welcoming, the mood is casual and relaxed, and the location is inspiring: the Merion is situated a block from Cape May's beautiful beach. Dinner is served 5-9pm (10pm on Saturdays). The Merion's Café menu features appetizers, panini and desserts and is served 8:30-10pm (9:30-11pm on Saturdays). And check out the $14.95 early evening specials before 5:30. Free parking and children's menu. Visit www.merioninn.com for reservations, menus, virtual tour, hours and events. *106 Decatur Street at Columbia Ave., (609) 884-8363.*

THE PELICAN CLUB

Panoramic views are rare in Cape May – Victorian architecture doesn't lend itself to such a thing. The spectacular exception lies on the sixth floor of the Marquis de Lafayette hotel, on Beach Avenue. This is where the Pelican Club restaurant lives, and it's a place you need to include in your Cape May itinerary. First of all, the food is wonderful. Highlights include the grilled Cuban rubbed pork chop with whipped sweet potatoes, plantain chips and red wine-infused pork jus, and the sauteed halibut with toasted almond herb crust, cauliflower and light curry cream. Even if you're not in the mood for dinner, the bar alone is worth the visit. You can gaze over the Atlantic, watching the dolphins frolic in the surf as you peruse a superb martini menu and an excellent beer list. And, of course, the wine list is exceptional, given that the Pelican Club is owned by the Craig family, who also have the acclaimed Washington Inn. *501 Beach Ave., (609) 884-3995, www.pelicanclubcapemay.com.*

TISHA'S FINE DINING

Some restaurants have an amazing location and decent food, some have a humdrum location and superb food, and then there are the select few that have an amazing location AND superb food. Tisha's for one. This gem is located next to Convention Hall right on the boardwalk and features the best-situated fine dining tables in town (the ones on the balcony are snapped up particularly quickly). The location isn't the only thing that makes Tisha's a special place to visit. Chef Paul Negro, who owns the restaurant with wife Jennifer, changes the menu regularly throughout the season, so you can keep coming back and never take this place for granted (as if). The food is New American with a strong Italian influence, which means you can expect some special pasta dishes as well as blackened and grilled fish dishes, paired with intriguing sauces, for which Tisha's has become well known since it opened in Cape May in 1994. *714 Beach Ave., (609) 884-9119, BYO, www.tishasfinedining.com.*

Photo courtesy of DJ Ardore, Restaurantpassion.com

THE UGLY MUG

The Ugly Mug isn't just a bar and restaurant – it's a local legend. A lot of folk in town have stories about memorable nights they've enjoyed here. While others have come and gone, changed names and changed owners, the Mug keeps going, attracting a mixture of locals (who might sit at the bar and discuss the 150lb tuna caught that day) and the tourists who keep coming back. The old place is looking good these days – owners Bob and Lisa Ransom recently spruced it up without losing any of its character. You can either eat in the restaurant itself (perfect for big groups and families) or at one of the tables that surround the bar – either way, you have a huge selection of appetizers, sandwiches, soups and salads to choose from. The photo was taken at the Froth-Blowing contest which has been taking place the last Sunday in August for the last 50 years – another example of the place the Mug holds in Cape May lore. *Washington St. Mall, (609) 884-4590 www.uglymugenterprises.com.*

UNCLE BILL'S PANCAKE HOUSE

Lines will begin forming outside Uncle Bill's Pancake House on summer weekend mornings. Why? Because the list of breakfast choices is enormous, the pancakes are wonderful and, well, it's just a very cool place to sit and enjoy a hearty start to the day. You can take a seat at the counter if you're alone and want to sit and read your paper in peace, or if you have company you'll want to settle into one of the booths that run around the perimeter of this circular building, which sits right across from the beach and which began its life as a cocktail bar for Congress Hall hotel in the 1950s. Wherever you sit, you're going to find something on this menu that sets you up for the day. Service is friendly and efficient and refills are plentiful. Eat at Uncle Bill's and you probably won't be doing too much thinking about lunch that day. *Beach Avenue & Perry, (609) 884-7199 and also at 3820 Bayshore Road, North Cape May, (609) 884-0066.*

VANTHIA'S

If there's such a thing as healthy soul food, then that's the best way to describe Vanthia's. You always feel like you're eating well here, but you also feel like you did when you were cooked dinner by your favorite aunt or grandmother – filled up and nourished. This is most likely because the ingredients at Vanthia's are fresh and wholesome, while the servings are huge. For instance, the Greek salad with pita points and chicken is a lunch feast that will keep you satisfied all day long, yet you'll still felt like you ate a healthy meal (you did). But while there's a Greek influence here (which accounts for the sensational salads), there's a whole lot more besides. Chef Luis Mercado, who runs the restaurant with wife Demetria (the Greek influence) is equally at home with flounder stuffed with crabmeat or filet mignon tail rolled in peppercorn. Finally, breakfast at Vanthia's is one of the best-kept secrets in town. *106 Sunset Boulevard, West Cape May, (609) 884-4020, www.vanthias.com.*

THE WASHINGTON INN

The Washington Inn is one of the founding fathers of fine dining in Cape May. And while other new establishments have embellished the town's reputation as a restaurant destination, the Washington Inn still stands as the benchmark for exquisite food and wines. There are five dining rooms, from lush summer patios to super-cozy fireside rooms, where you can practically taste the oaks and fruits from the restaurant's magnificent wine cellar, the finest in southern Jersey. And we should probably mention the food. The grilled duck breast and confit of duck leg with parsnip, turnip and Yukon mashed, braised red cabbage and blackberry jus is fantastic, as is the butter-poached cold water lobster tail with rock shrimp risotto in blood-orange vinaigrette. This is a classically cool dining experience and you should dress for the part – this isn't a shorts and T-shirt place. Make an effort – the food, wine and service are well worth it. *801 Washington Street, (609) 884-5697, www.washingtoninn.com.*

WATERS EDGE

This is a place where they take food seriously, but life less so, which means you're in for a great culinary experience AND a lot of fun, thanks to general manager Ed Collins and his crew. The best way to enjoy Waters Edge is to allow time for a cocktail at the bar – expertly tended by Gary LaRue – before you sample the menu that many believe paved the way for Cape May's innovative cuisine. Chef/owner Neil Elsohn began experimenting when he first opened the restaurant in 1987 and he's never stopped. This is American cuisine at its most creative. Some highlights – fluke filled with jumbo lump crabmeat, shitake mushrooms and mascarpone and the incredible blackened diver scallops with caramel-preserved ginger glaze. And we haven't even mentioned the view yet – big windows open on to the tranquil beach at the eastern end of town, which has a more spiritual feel than the more touristy beaches further west. *Beach Ave., at Pittsburgh, (609) 884-1717, www.watersedgerestaurant.com.*

ZOE'S BEACHFRONT EATERY

Every beachfront should have a Zoe's – here are three reasons why you should go there. 1. BREAKFAST – you need nourishment to give you the energy to lie and snooze under the sun all day, and Zoe's has delicious homemade pancakes that are probably the cheapest in town. 2. LUNCH – you don't want to stray far from the beach when your beautifully-tanned tummy starts to rumble, so you walk across Beach Avenue and check out the freshly-made sandwiches, hoagies, salads and burgers. 3. DINNER – maybe you skipped lunch and you realize as you walk off the beach that you can't wait until you've showered and changed and you want to eat right NOW, so you go to Zoe's, sit on the patio, order a grilled chicken caesar and enjoy that wonderful late-afternoon light. Wait, there's a fourth reason: Zoe's has great veggie burgers and sandwiches for the under-served vegetarians who wander the streets of Cape May looking for sustenance. *Beach Ave., next to the movie theater, (609) 884-1233.*

DEPOT MARKET CAFE

If you ever go to a Chinese restaurant in Chinatown in New York or Philadelphia and you see lots of Chinese folks eating there, it makes you feel confident about the place, right? If the locals like it, then it must be good. So it goes with the Depot Market. Go in here and you'll find discerning Cape May natives all year round. There is nothing fancy going on here – just great food done well. The biggest seller in summer is usually the chicken caesar salad, pictured above, but this place is busy every month of the year. Hot sandwiches include barbeque pork & cheese, roast beef, Italian sweet sausage with parmesan, Depot crab cake and chicken gorgonzola. Main courses include lasagna, meatloaf, chicken parmesan, stuffed pork chops and chicken pot pie. The Depot also claims to serve the largest stuffed baked potatoes in the world. Or just stop in for a coffee and a homemade brownie, cookie or cake. *409 Elmira St., (609) 884-8030.*

A CA MIA A superb northern Italian restaurant where the menu is as alluring as the location itself – the perfect people-watching spot on the mall. Highlights among the entrees include the heavenly Jersey flounder roulade, stuffed with crabmeat, sundried tomatoes, black olives, cream cheese and fresh basil. Or how about the smoked fish sampler, a wonderful appetizer, served with horseradish, mustard sauce and roasted pepper. A Ca Mia recently expanded and now has a deli next door, which sells the finest, freshest meats, salads and cheeses, should you wish to concoct your own feast. *524 Washington Mall, (609) 884-8030.*

FRESCO'S

This charming restaurant has been named the Best Fine Italian restaurant for thirteen years in a row by the readers of New Jersey Monthly magazine. No surprise, given that it's operated by the same people who have 410 Bank Street next door. Fresco's is located in an 1880 Victorian cottage that's been designed to look and feel like a trattoria in Tuscany. The seafoods and rich homemade pastas are inspired by the south of Italy, while the north is represented by the elegant sauces and veal. Whatever meal you choose, you need to begin with the famous garlic bread. *412 Bank Street, (609) 884-0366.*

SHOPPING

ANDREW'S

On walking through the door, Andrew's appears, at first glance, to be a jewelry store. But as your eyes browse the walls and display cases of this pretty little shop you realize there's more – a lot more – going on. Yes, there IS a beautiful collection of estate jewelry, but there is also an eclectic mixture of antiques and collectibles that will appeal to both sexes and most age groups, too. On any given day at Andrew's there could be any manner of beautiful things – on the days we visited, there were gorgeous stained-glass panels, a great selection of antique men's watches, some old toy cars from the 30s and 40s, and some wonderful hand-colored photographs from the 1920s or 30s by Wallace Nutting, regarded as the "Father of American Antiques." In short, a fantastic collection of antique Americana. The music in the background was cool, too, and guess what, that's for sale also – check out the mellow, loungy CDs on a rack on the wall. *318 Washington St. Mall, 898-7755.*

THE BIRD HOUSE OF CAPE MAY
Victorian architecture for birds?! Why not? They have feel-ings, too, and as it turns out, exquisite tastes. But those tastes vary, which is why this great store has bird houses in colonial, traditional and eclectic styles, in case your peeps aren't feeling the Victorian vibe. There's also a complete selection of feed-ers, recirculating ponds and baths. But not everything's for the birds. For humans, there are garden accents, wrought-iron pieces, nature-inspired home decor and gifts for nature-lovers of all ages. From the local scene, they have original art work, shore birds by Cape May County decoy carvers and the Jingle Bird Collection – hand-painted replicas of south Jersey folk art. Open year-round since 1995, The Bird House of Cape May has a must-see assortment like none you've seen back home. *Happily nestled at 109 Sunset Boulevard, West Cape May, (609) 898-8871, www.birdhouseofcapemay.com*

CapeMay.com

TodayInCapeMay.com   *CapeMayRealEstate.com*

CAPE PUBLISHING

Everybody who knows Cape May knows CapeMay.com, the on-line magazine published by Cape Publishing. But they produce some top quality printed pieces too! "Cape May in Pictures" is a series of postcards available in local stores. Great for mailing or collecting, each packet of 12 cards portrays Cape May in a different light. The Classic postcard set has beautiful new pictures of idyllic Cape May. Victorian Cape May, Seaside Cape May and Uniquely Cape May are the other thematic collections, each emphasizing a specific aspect of the town. While you're shopping for these Limited Edition collections, be sure to ask for Cape Publishing's children's sticker books and the full-color edition of *Sentinel of the Jersey Cape*, the story of the Cape May lighthouse. And if you miss anything by the time you get back home, you can order through www.CapeMay.com, where every day, all year long, the beauty of Cape May is only a click away. *513 Washington Mall, (609) 898-4500.*

CAROLINE BOUTIQUE
Cape May's most stylish and hip boutique, with clothing made by contemporary designers using mostly natural fibers. Pop into this 130-year-old carriage house and treat yourself to a session of retail therapy with clothes that will make you feel dressy yet casual, sophisticated yet relaxed, and just darn right fabulous, without overdoing it, of course! Eileen Fisher, Only Hearts, Michaels Stars, Ella Moss, Grassroots and Sanctuary are just a sampling of labels carried in the two-story upscale boutique. Check out the funky accessories, unusual jewelry and cool tees. If you're ever in the Florida Keys, visit their sister store Blue at 718 Caroline Street, Key West. *400 Carpenter's Lane, (609) 884-5055.*

FABRIC OUTLET

Hundreds of yards of in-stock first-quality designer fabric and trim-
mings are sold in this neat little store in Cape May Court House.
Designs include a full line of "sunbrella", and they're all discounted up
to 75%. Other discounted designer lines represented include
Kravet, Laura Ashley, F. Schumacher, Dura Lee, Waverly, Grammercy,
B&F, Artmark, Suburban and Peachtree. Find fabric and supplies for
quilting here as well as custom-cut foam, batting, and sewing supplies.
Not sure how to sew? Fabric Outlet offers classes in sewing, quilting,
no-sew decorating, and interior design. For home, there's a full line of
furniture by Kravet, Laura Ashley, Maine Cottage, British Traditions
and Outdoor Designs. Buy accessories and art, custom and semi-
custom linens and bedding. The store also sells gifts, handbags, and
jewelry. Topping it all off is a full service design center by Muse Three
Designs, including new construction, rental design, and interior rede-
sign services. *701 Route 9 S, Cape May Court House, (609) 465-6701.*

MADAME'S PORT

We defy anyone to walk in this store and not fall in love at least five or six times. It could be with the Bali chair, hand-woven with sea grass in Indonesia; the wood/stainless steel tic tac toe set; the wonderfully-minimalist Edo lounge chair from Italy; the hanging cylinder lamp; the small mango wood vase; the colorful sushi sets; the folding rocking chair with soft leather magazine satchel (*especially* the folding rocking chair – it's irresistible). Madame's Port has furniture for the living room, the bedroom, home decor items, unique gifts, and jewelry. Owners Steve and Pat Smarro have scoured the world to find this stuff – Mexico, Canada, Thailand, Indonesia, India, Kenya, China, Nepal, Germany, the UK, France... it's like a United Nations of beautiful things! The decor and careful lighting means it's a great place to either escape the 95-degree heat in mid-August or to enjoy a cozy retail therapy session on a wet spring or winter afternoon. *311 Washington St. Mall, (609) 884-5858, www.madames-port.com.*

THE ORIGINAL FUDGE KITCHEN

In 1972, brothers Joe and Paul Bogle got together to start a fudge shop in North Wildwood. More than 30 years later, their insistence on homespun quality and values has turned their little idea into a hugely-successful operation. Their famous cream fudge is made in copper kettles, whipped by hand the old fashioned way, using only country-fresh cream, pure cane sugar and the very finest natural ingredients. The Original Fudge Kitchen has a dizzying selection of goods to choose from – there are 18 flavors of fudge alone, as well as a mouthwatering range of candies, chocolates and confections. So whether you want a treat for yourself, want to spoil family or friends or are looking for a tasty holiday gift – St. Valentine's, Easter, Christmas, whenever! – visit one of their two locations in Cape May (there are others in the Wildwoods, Stone Harbor and Ocean City) or shop online. *513 Washington St. Mall and 728 Beach Ave., on the promenade, 884-2834, 800-23-FUDGE, www.fudgekitchens.com.*

SWAIN'S ACE HARDWARE

For a business to survive more than 100 years is unusual. For it to remain an independently-owned and operated company in the same family for four generations is virtually unheard of. But so it goes at Swain's, the town's venerable hardware store. The gentleman in the dungarees is Charles A. Swain, who opened a small tin roofing store on this site in 1896 and whose great-granddaughter Terri Swain is the proprietor these days. Terri took over from her father, Charles "Bud" Swain, who still comes to work every day, following in the footsteps of his father, Charles "Nick" Swain, who up until his death in December, 2003 – at the age of 100 – had worked at the store every day. Swain's is a place where, as the saying goes, everyone knows your name and where experienced assistants will actually approach the customer and offer help. If you're tired of playing Spot-the-Assistant in any of the hardware behemoths, you'll know how good that feels. *305 Jackson St., (609) 884-8578.*

UP IN SMOKE

As you step inside this unique place, the textures and aromas transport you to a time long past. The founders have crafted a vision of superior customer attention, unsurpassed quality of products, and rich, opulent surroundings in which to enjoy them. Purveying the finest selection of premium cigars, accessories, and distinctive gifts – all beautifully displayed in the surroundings of exotic woods and stunning artwork – is only the beginning. The attention to quality and professionalism brought Up In Smoke into partnership with manufacturers of fine accessories, such as S.T. Dupont, Parker, Colibri, Lampe Berger, Thomas Kinkade, Roger & Gallet and Truefitt & Hill. Never wavering from the standards established by its owners, Up In Smoke is defined by the men and women who enjoy the finer things in life. *479 West Perry St., West Cape May, (609) 884-5009.*

VICTORIOUS

The Hobo and other handbags sold here are so stylish you'll want to walk out with all of them. Well, at least that was how we felt during our visit. Perhaps because they're made with light, soft leather and crafted into fashionable styles, big carryalls or sleek rectangles to name just a couple. In addition to fabulous purses, Victorious carries upscale popular jewelry lines like Sorrelli and Lunch at the Ritz, but they specialize in antique wedding bands and engagement rings. Listen to gemologist and manager Jen Papendick and learn about the tradition of wearing your wedding band first, then your engagement ring second (it's closer to your heart). You'll be impressed by her knowledge of the precious stones. Or just stroll in to buy the gorgeous Beach Glass line of bracelets and necklaces in sea foamy or muted red colors. Victorious also stocks some quality-crafted furniture. It's challenging not to take home a large bag of goodies from this classy store. *Congress Hall shops, (609) 898-1777.*

WANDERLUST

"Bring a lil' Hula Home" is the theme behind this new store, which is retail heaven for anyone who loves *Coastal Living* magazine and who lives at the beach – or dreams about it. Wanderlust, which occupies a gorgeous old wooden building on quiet Jefferson Street, is one of the best things that's happened to Cape May shopping. There's island-inspired furniture from Palecek, which you'll see all over the hit TV show, *The OC*; tightly-woven rattans and wickers from Selamat, for a rich look, with leather or cloth cushions; rugs by Global Home in all sorts of colors and fabrics (even leather); linens and bath products by Tommy Bahama; Hawaii's first bedding line of tropical prints by Dean Miller; and "Bedding for Beachgoers" by Uhula. If you dream of a hammock (and who doesn't) Wanderlust has the coolest line you've ever seen. Plus there are string lites, citronella candles, throw pillows, lanterns and more. Bring a little beach house to your house! *609 Jefferson St., (609) 884-0488.*

WHALE'S TALE

Searching for lavender jade or lemon quartz? Maybe you are and you just didn't know it yet. In any event, you are in for a treat at Whale's Tale, with their extensive selection of handcrafted jewelry featuring unusual gemstones, pearls and dichroic glass. If you are a collector of seashells you'll appreciate the world-class assortment of specimen shells. Wherever you wander in this Cape May institution (and we mean that in the best possible way), you'll likely find something unique and beautiful. Treat yourself to a fragrant bath and body product from Crabtree & Evelyn. Prepare to get lost as you discover a room filled with a spectacular variety of greeting cards, gift wrap and imported paper goods. And there's more. Educational toys or children's books? Something for a nature lover? A classy Cape May souvenir? Don't miss Whale's Tale, a place that people have been seeking out for 30 years. *312 Washington Mall, (609) 884-4808, www.WhalesTaleCapeMay.com.*

ENVIRONS

Looking for superior products for the bath and home? Walk on over to Congress Hall hotel, stroll into Environs and prepare to be impressed. You'll discover Cape May's premier lifestyles shop, specializing in European accents and upscale wares that aren't normally seen on this island. In fact, Environs exclusively stocks the L'Occitane body and home fragrance collections. There is also original art, handcrafted jewelry and funky finds like a bin full of chic brown baseballs. The Santa Maria Novella line of home fragrances and fine soaps from Florence make great hostess gifts, as do the Votivo candles. There's even a row of gorgeous silky ribbons to choose from for the perfect finishing touch. *251 Beach Ave., (609) 884-5252, 888-884-5252.*

THE FLYING FISH STUDIO

If you've visited your share of charming seaside towns you'll have noticed (if you pay attention to such things) that a lot of the T-shirts are similar. There are generic boating and fishing motifs and you get the feeling that there's a factory somewhere with someone sitting and stamping on the names of towns in the appropriate space. And the point of all this? At The Flying Fish, every single T-shirt is home-made and home-designed. Many of them celebrate Cape May life and traditions – the beach, local festivals, um, *Exit Zero* newspaper (Flying Fish is an exclusive stockist of our T-shirts), so you can be sure you're taking home a unique slice of local life. The store also sells other creative clothing and accessories. *Park Blvd, (609) 884-2760, www.theflyingfishstudio.com.*

TOMMY'S FOLLY

If you love Congress Hall, Cape May's most magnificent hotel, then you're going to want to visit its little gift shop which is packed with top-quality souvenirs from the hotel and a whole lot more besides. Bearing the Congress Hall logo in various forms are bathrobes, pajamas, T-shirts, fleeces, baby's bibs, baseball caps and visors, flip-flops, golf umbrellas and travel-size umbrellas, beach towels, purses, jigsaw puzzles, tableware, linens and all sorts of fun stuff. The shop also has a great selection of classic rainy day games and you can stock up here for the beach with magazines, sunglasses and other little necessary items. *251 Beach Ave., 888-944-1816, www.congresshall.com.*

VINTAGE COTTAGE

This new shabby chic shop offers a charming selection of new home and garden items and "painted past" vintage furniture. Owner Caroline Ranoia paints all the furniture, as well as the murals – that's her breezy blue sky covering a good portion of the walls. There are stencils from over 25 designers ranging from whimsical to sophisticate. Paints and supplies are for sale too. Her goal is to "inspire and create images in your home that were just dreams." Group stenciling classes are offered, or consult with Caroline to give your room a new look with a "use what you have" philosophy. The store also has appealing French accents like clocks and toile memo boards. *600 Park Blvd, (609) 898-4300. www.vintagecottage.com.*

BATH TIME

Indulge in Mandarin Mambo fruit cream soap, Sweet Olive and Cedar Italian Midani, or try any of the other 250 varieties for sale. There are choices galore for all bath products, including Cape May Blends, Bath Time's own line of bath and body products that you scent yourself. There are also bath & body products by Burt's Bees, Essential Elements and Lather. *223 Jackson Street, (609) 884-9234, 800-424-BATH, www.bathtime.com.*

BAY SPRINGS ALPACAS

Cape May has many surprises, and this is one of them. Near the end of beautiful New Engalnd Road lies an alpaca farm, where Warren and Barbara Nuessle live what they call the "alpaca lifestyle" – quiet and simple. You can visit at weekends and see how alpaca fiber is spun into yarn, and shop at the store, which has sweaters, vests, scarves, hats, gloves, blankets and alpaca miniatures. *542 New England Rd., (609) 884-0563, www.BaySpringsAlpacas.com.*

BEACH CRITTERS

Moms and grandmoms love shopping here – it carries cute bits of everything for boys and girls aged infant to preteens. The clothes go from bathing suits to party dresses with accessories like socks and cute little headbands. Brands include Lilly Pulitzer, Zutano, April Cornell, Roxy, and Baby LuLu. For a supercute look, buy baby's outfit here and get mom's to match at sister store 39 Degrees. *Washington Commons, (609) 898-8550.*

GUARDIAN

The atmosphere in this oasis is comfortable, personal and in common perspective so that all who enter can relax and discover the power to reclaim their birthright to live a life of mystery, purpose, and magic. Guardian is your cosmic resource for spiritual and energy healing with essences like angels, affirmations, aromatherapy, books, crystals, Celtic items, candles, fairies, and jewelry. *221 Jackson Street, (609) 884-6179.*

KATE'S FLOWER SHOP

Many of Cape May's top B&Bs and restaurants are decorated with Kate's cut flower bouquets. But she says she owes her success to her staff, Anita, Sheila, and Rich. "I couldn't do any of this if these guys weren't here," she says. You can walk in and purchase a fresh cut bouquet from the coolers or have flowers delivered anywhere in the country. Open Monday 10-4, Tuesday to Friday 9-5, Saturday 9-12. Closed Sundays. *600 Park Blvd. (609) 884-6181.*

OUT OF THE PAST

If your grandmother had great taste, was a hoarder, then turned her attic inside out one day, the contents would look like the inside of this little store. Everywhere you look are lovely surprises – china, clothing, books, trinkets. And it can't go without saying that a book from the 1930s provided the inspiration for this guide that you're reading – isn't that reaon enough to visit? *394 Myrtle St., corner of Perry, (609) 884-3357, www.outofthepast.us.*

SUNSTRUCK

There's a breezy tiki atmosphere here that'll send you to Hawaii without leaving Cape May. Owners Emilie and Kathy carry the largest selection of bathing suits for juniors, women, and kids in town. Designer lines range from Guess, OP, Rusty, and Bebe, to Ralph Lauren, Tommy Bahama, Jantzen, and Tommy Hilfiger. There are also flip-flops from Sanuk and FloJos and other beach essentials. *Washington Commons, next to the Acme. (609) 898-3850.*

39 DEGREES

This clothing and accessories store is described as "preppy chic" by owner Nancy Connolly. It's one of only two in the area to carry Lilly Pulitzer. Other designers icnlude James Perse, Love Life, and Lisa Curran swim. Accessories by Jane Fox and Kiss My Feet shoes will complete your ensemble. Go for preppy closet essentials like monogrammed tees and whale belts. For men, there's surfwear by Quiksilver Edition. *Congress Hall shops, (609) 884-6677.*

ART DECOR GALLERY

If you're the kind of person who could spend a long time paging through really old copies of National Geographic or 100-year-old nature and science encyclopedias and you're also the kind of person who would emit a little gasp of excitement if you saw a bunch of old prints of birds, flowers, whales, sharks and butterflies then, first of all, you're NOT a loser. And secondly, you're going to love Art Decor Gallery. There's all of this in here, plus beautiful prints of Victorian ladies, old ships and maps and meteorological illustrations, like a particularly appealing print from an old German encyclopedia that shows all the different cloud formations with their names in Latin (which is good for impressing someone as you stroll through town pointing out all the lovely cirrus clouds around the lighthouse and how you hope there aren't any nimbus clouds on the horizon). *31 Perry Street, Carpenter's Square Mall, (609) 898-7488.*

McDOWELL'S GALLERY

"Most customers who come in for the first time are in awe of the ambiance," says employee Pat, and it's easy to see why. Even from the outside the old brick building is impressive and will catch your eye as you stroll down the Washington Street Mall. The building's history dates back to 1895, when it was a bank, and most of the woodwork in there today is still original. McDowell's sells unique gifts on the first floor, while up the wooden staircase on the second floor is an art gallery. There are so many items displayed that you may need to come in more than once to ensure you haven't missed anything. There are lamps, furniture, floral arrangements, art prints, and stained glass for the home. For gifts choose from cologne, jewelry, scrimshaw, candles, and potpourri. Chances are good that you will leave here with something you love. *526 Washington Street, corner of Ocean, (609) 884-0430.*

MP MYERS PHOTOGRAPHY

Take a walk around Mary Pat Myers' beautiful studio in the heart of the Historic District and you'll probably find yourself thinking two things: 1. I want wide-beamed wood-paneled walls *exactly* like she has; 2. In which century were these photographs taken? As for 1., the walls have been like that for a century or more. As for 2., you're right, Mary Pats' photographs DO have a timeless, classic quality. She photographs only in natural light, during the hour before sundown (which doesn't do much for her social life in summer). She opened her Cape May studio in 1990 after falling in love with the town, and left the computer business world behind for ever. These days Mary Pat shoots around 35 weddings per year but children's and family portraits are what she loves to do most. Parents have been known to cry at her portraits of their children (and we mean that in a purely positive way). *611 Jefferson Street, (609) 884-6354, www.mpmyersphotography.com.*

OCEAN STREET GALLERY

Though it's called a gallery, you will see this as more of a high-end gift shop, selling unique items and specializing in sterling, marcasite and amber, a best seller that's imported from the Baltic Sea area. Ocean Street Gallery also carries limited-production stained glass designed by local artists. So if you are looking for a mosaic piece of furniture, a special piece of jewelry, a unique gift, or perhaps a small remembrance of your trip to beautiful Cape May, stop in and be convinced. *208 Ocean Street, (609) 884-0088.*

TIDES OF TIME GALLERY®

In the spring of 1994, outsider artist Corey Gilbert stumbled upon an ancient hall of records, hidden near Cape May. The stone carvings of Mayan, Phoenician, Oriental, Easter Island, Peruvian and Egyptian heads, maps, weights and calendar dates inspired him to borrow photographic equipment and begin to document the artifacts. His interest in photography grew and coincided with him moving into a little cottage on the beach. Camera in hand, Corey began capturing incredible images of lightning storms (some so violent that you realize Corey has serious *cojones*, as they say in Spanish, as well as a great eye), kaleidoscopic sunsets and other Cape May natural wonders. This led him to open the Tides of Time.com Gallery and Cape Maya.com museum and his name has since become synonymous with remarkable environmental photography. *31 Perry Street, Carpenter's Square Mall, 884-3306, 884-2916, www.tidesoftime.com.*

WASHINGTON COMMONS GALLERY

Paintings of all shapes and sizes, with the emphasis on high quality hand-painted oils on canvas, line the walls and floors of this spacious gallery. Many of them are custom-painted by local, national, and international artists exclusively for the gallery. The artists are highly-skilled, dedicated professionals, not just casual artists according to owner Pierce Herbst. He's been in the art business for 23 years and knows what customers are looking for – the highest quality and the best value. Come and see Armenian phenom, Artur Saryan, paint his masterpieces in the window. If you like what you see, you can buy originals or reprints of his work. The gallery's hand-finished frames are the finest available and come factory direct. Likewise, all artwork is studio artwork. There is no middleman – prices throughout Washington Commons Gallery are "wholesale to the public." *Washington and Ocean Streets, (609) 884-1880, www.gallerysales@att.net.*

AQUA TRAILS

Imagine paddling slowly through wetlands, a night light on your kayak pointing out your position to your fellow paddlers, though you're also illuminated by the full moon that's risen on this summer's night. Meanwhile, Ospreys circle overhead and the endangered black skimmers search for grass shrimp on the surface of the water, while on the banks, oystercatchers are roosting. This is perhaps the highlight of Aqua Trails' program – the full moon tour, which runs July to September. But any time is a good time to investigate Cape May's wetlands. As you wind your way through this landscape, you'll see and hear flora and fauna in the air, on the land, on the water, and under the water. Aqua Trails also runs two daily guided tours, expertly led by Aqua Trails owner (and local biology teacher) Jeff Martin. There is also a new sunset tour twice a week, on Tuesdays and Saturdays. Or you can rent a single or double kayak and go your own way. *Ocean Drive, (609) 884-5600, www.aquatrails.com.*

CAPE FITNESS

Owners George and Elise Rohana and Jessica Lang (*not* the one who got all her clothes ripped off by King Kong) believe fitness experience and knowledge is the best reason to visit their gym, whether you're a weekender, summer dweller, or a local. "We pride ourselves on our background and education, not only as owners but as instructors," says Jessica. Their six instructors lead a number of different classes. There's Spinning, Body Blast (Total body conditioning), Abs, Functional Training or Sports Specific Training. Cape Fitness flexes its knowledge by providing clients with both one-on -one and group training, children's classes, and nutritional and weight-loss consultations. For a challenging solo work out select from equipment including Icarian weight machines, free weights, EFX, Treadmills, stationary bikes, rowing machines and stairmasters. *600 Park Boulevard, (609) 898-1515.*

CAPE MAY WINERY

The nine acres of land that the Cape May Winery calls home is situated between the Atlantic Ocean and the Delaware Bay, making it a perfect location for the grape vines to soak in the sun and grow in the sandy soil. Started some twenty years ago, the winery is busy producing award-winning red and white wines, including Merlot, Chardonnay, Pinot Grigio, Cabernet Sauvignon, Riesling, and Blush. Stop in the nicely-appointed tasting room for a sample or two and to pick up neat little gifts for the wine lovers on your list. There are tours offered weekly by the Mid-Atlantic Center for the Arts (884-5404) and if you like what you see (we're guessing you will), call up 884-5697 and ask for Randall. He's the event coordinator for the winery and will help you plan your wedding or any other special event in style. *709 Townbank Road, (609) 884-1169, www.capemaywinery.com.*

MID-ATLANTIC CENTER FOR THE ARTS (MAC)

Cape May's leader in heritage tourism, MAC offers a year-round schedule of special events, as well as walking, boat, trolley and house tours, including tours of Cape May's only Victorian house museum, the 1879 Emlen Physick Estate, photographed above. The 1876 Carriage House at the Physick Estate houses the Carriage House Gallery with its changing exhibits, the Twinings Tearoom, and a tea-themed Gallery Shop. MAC also restored and operates the 1859 Cape May Lighthouse, located in Cape May Point State Park. Visitors can climb the 199 steps of the lighthouse for a breathtaking view of the Atlantic Ocean and Delaware Bay. Major special events include spring's Cape May Music Festival, October's Victorian Week, the Food & Wine Festival in September, Christmas in Cape May, Sherlock Holmes Weekends, and a variety of summertime programs and events geared for family fun. *1048 Washington St., (609) 884-5404, 800-275-4278, www.capemaymac.org.*

MOREY'S PIERS

Morey's Piers' three action-packed amusement piers and waterparks feature a wide variety of thrill rides, family rides and attractions – all located on America's Boardwalk in Wildwood. With more than 100 rides and attractions, including seven world-class roller-coasters, a 160-foot high ferris wheel and more than 30 kiddie rides, there's something for everyone. Two beachfront Raging Waters waterparks feature water slides, speed slides, endless winding rivers and cool refreshing pools, plus two exclusive children's play areas, Bonsai Beach and Camp Kid-Tastrophe. To satisfy your Boardwalk food cravings, you'll find Curley's fries, funnel cakes, pizza and full-course dinners with wait staff at Jumbo's Seafood Eatery. The new picnic facility, Rendezvous Beach, is perfect for corporate picnics, family reunions and parties. *Morey's Piers, Spencer, Schellenger and 25th Ave.; Raging Waters waterparks, Schellenger and 25th Ave., (609) 522-3900, www.moreyspiers.com*

NORTH BEACH HEALTH CLUB

A gym can be an intimidating experience for some folks. Will it be full of muscleheads grunting and groaning to pounding music? Will you need to be in half-decent shape before you even show up? That's why North Beach calls itself the friendly, feelgood gym. As owner Mark Chamberlain says, "People want somewhere they can come and work out, maybe change their lives, maybe just feel a little bit better about themselves. It sounds corny, but we really do feel like a family." That's why tourists keep coming back here, because they're made to feel part of that family, and daily, weekly and monthly passes make it viable for them to stay in shape while they vacation at the Shore. North Beach offers 11 different classes from a team of qualified instructors led by Becky Chamberlain, one of the most experienced and sought-after group instructors in the state. There is also tanning and childcare facilities. *Bayshore Mall, next to Bayshore 8 cinema, 886-4842, www.northbeachgym.com.*

SUNSET BEACH

One of the enduring Cape May traditions is the lowering of the American flag at Sunset Beach, to the strains of Kate Smith singing *God Bless America*. So it might be a little kitschy for some tastes, but that's the point – this is classic Americana. Besides, the sunsets here are truly spectacular – weather permitting, you shouldn't even think about leaving Cape May without witnessing the little scene that plays out here in front of the Concrete Ship that sank here in 1926 (you have to wonder why anyone would ever have thought it was a good idea to build a ship out of concrete). And don't worry if you think your kids will be over the whole sunset thing in two minutes flat – there's plenty to do here besides staring at the magnificent display in the sky. There are three stores full of all sorts of novelty gifts and goods, and the Sunset Beach Grill serves up burgers, dogs and other American staples. *Sunset Beach, (609) 884-7095, www.sunsetbeachnj.com.*

CAPE MAY DAY SPA

Want to make this the most revitalizing and relaxing trip you've ever had here? Book a treat at Cape May Day Spa. Highly recommended is The Victorian Experience – you and your significant other soak in the oversized whirlpool tub then enjoy a side-by-side full body massage, all by candlelight. There are dozens of other ways to feel fantastic – the spa offers massages, from shiatsu to reflexology, LaStone to Swedish, plus facials, body treatments, pedicures and manicures. *607 Jefferson St., (609) 898-1003, www.capemaydayspa.com.*

THE MASSAGE CENTER

The nine therapists on staff perform a variety of massages including Swedish, Deep Tissue, Neuro Muscular, Reiki, and Massage Facial. If you're hurting from too much surfing/biking/partying, head on over the bridge because treating clients in pain is a specialty. They get referrals from chiropractors whose clients are suffering from tight muscles, sciatica, carpal tunnel, headaches, and back pain. It's soothing to know that owner Penny Graham's goal is achieved when a client "walks in having pain and walks out pain free." The Center recently moved from Rio Grande to the Bolero Hotel in Wildwood and for a small fee, clients can use the hotel's gym, pool, steam room, sauna and Jacuzzi. Open seven days and nights. *Bolero Hotel, 3320 Atlantic Ave., Wildwood, (609) 522-9220.*

TOUCH & GO MASSAGE

Just because you're on vacation doesn't mean you don't need to be de-stressed – what's more stressful than trying to be happy for a whole week! Luckily, certified massage therapist Kathy Kint of Touch and Go Massage is ready to spring into action. Kathy will bring massage to you – just relax and enjoy your massage in your B&B, vacation rental, or hotel room. Kathy brings everything – aromatherapy, music, table, sheets... and her healing hands. Kathy has a new studio in North Cape May if your place is not suitable for massage. She does a wonderful integrated massage using techniques such as Swedish, Deep Tissue and Trigger Point. Touch and Go also offers Massage Therapy Facials and Sound Healing. (609) 972-6260, www.touchandgomassage.com.

TURDO VINEYARDS

DID you know that Cape May's southern climate is ideal for growing superb wines? The proof is in the tasting so come and see for yourself at Turdo Vineyards, producers of Turis wines. This family-owned company has a large variety to choose from, including award-winning Pinot Grigio and Merlot, plus Chardonnay, Pinot Noir, Cabernet Sauvignon and more. Cheese and wine tastings can be arranged by appointment, so please give Salvatore or Sara Turdo a call and spend a delightful afternoon enjoying authentic southern Italian hospitality. *3911 Bayshore Road, North Cape May, near the Cape May-Lewes ferry, (609) 898-3424, www.turdovineyards.com.*

CONGRESS HALL

In the summer of 2002, Cape May's grand old lady returned to her glory days after a remarkable $25 million renovation by the hotel's new owners. This is where four U.S. presidents stayed, and you can still feel the majesty of the place as you stroll through the lobby or walk the colonnaded veranda. Congress Hall has 104 rooms, many with ocean views and all of them decorated with the relaxed elegance that runs through the building, and five luxury suites. The hotel is a four-acre playground overlooking the Atlantic with all the amenities you need for a relaxing, fun vacation. There is a restaurant, room service, cocktail lounge, nightclub, pool and beach cabana serving food and drinks, a fitness room, full-service spa, and boutique stores in the lobby. The magnificent 4,000-square-foot ballroom is a regular venue for weddings and the hotel also has first-class executive conferencing facilities. *251 Beach Ave., (609) 884-8421, 888-944-1816, www.congresshall.com.*

THE FAIRTHORNE

Innkeepers Diane and Ed Hutchinson warmly welcome you to their romantic old whaling captain's home in the heart of the Historic District. This 1892 Colonial Revival-style inn features a gracious wraparound veranda where sumptuous breakfasts are served on pleasant mornings and stress-relieving rockers offer afternoon relaxation. Each day Diane and Ed invite you to gather for tasty snacks, fresh-baked cookies, with tea and coffee on cool days, iced tea and lemonade on summer days. In the evening, relax on the verandah and watch horse-drawn carriages tour the streets or sip a glass of sherry by a crackling fire before turning in for the night. The Fairthorne is beautifully decorated in period style without being too frilly or formal. Guestrooms are appointed with a seamless blend of fine antiques and contemporary comforts, including air conditioning, mini-fridges and TV, plus gas log fireplaces in some rooms. *111-115 Ocean Street, (609) 884-8791, 800-438-8742, www.fairthorne.com.*

ACCOMMODATION

JOHN F. CRAIG HOUSE

This beautiful home, built in 1850 with a Carpenter Gothic Victorian expansion in 1866, provides the true Victorian-era experience, with today's comforts. However, there is a twist – innkeepers Chip and Barbara Masemore feel that "everyone should be just plain silly sometimes" (we couldn't agree more) and it shows. Expect to see collections of bawdy ladies (not in person, we hasten to add), prewar Lionel trains, toys and other randomly-placed objects of intrigue. The inn offers open porches for warmer days, glassed-in porches and the warm glow of a fireplace in the magnificent parlor for cooler seasons. The beach, shopping mall and fine dining restaurants are a block away. Chip says they are all within "a seven iron," but we recommend you don't challenge him on this assertion. The city fathers, never mind fellow innkeepers, may not appreciate balls whirling through the streets of the Historic District. *609 Columbia Ave., (609) 884-0100, 877-544-0314, www.johnfcraig.com.*

ACCOMMODATION

THE LONGFELLOW GUEST HOUSE

Staying in the Longfellow Guest House is the perfect way to enjoy your Cape May vacation with family and friends. This lovely home has remained in the same family for its entire life – 153 years so far – and that's not something you can say about many, if any homes in Cape May. Located on the town's oldest residential street, the house is nestled in the heart of the Victorian district, within walking distance to the beaches, shopping areas and the best Victorian architecture in the country. Features include private parking, rear deck, front porch, Victorian amenities and modern conveniences. And the Longfellows recently added high-speed internet access, complimentary beach tags, a beach box and beach chairs. For helpful details and more photos it's recommended you visit the Longfellow Guest House's rather stylish and useful website. You can also email them at guide@longfellowhouse.com. *652 Hughes Street, (609) 884-3482, www.longfellowhouse.com.*

POOR RICHARD'S INN

Harriett Sosson doesn't run her B&B the way most people do. First of all she's really an artist (a talented one) more than a business-woman. This explains why she won't let you take a room if she thinks you won't be happy here (no soup for you!) and why she won't charge anywhere near what she ought to for a wonderful eight-room Victorian on gorgeous Jackson Street, less than a min-ute's walk to Cape May's main beach. So here's the deal – if you're a relaxed and thoughtful person you might just get to enjoy the best accommodation bargain in town. However, if you're expecting flat-screen TVs in your room, forget it. Harriett DOES have TVs, but they were all made around the time Michael J. Fox was hamming it on *Family Ties*. She does have basic cable, but if you're Harriett's kind of customer, you'd much rather enjoy the house's eclectic atmosphere, good conversation and breezy porches. *17 Jackson Street, (609) 884-3536, www.poorrichardsinn.com.*

THE SOUTHERN MANSION

This premier Cape May bed and breakfast offers large, luxurious, and romantic accommodations with a rich history. Built in the historic district circa 1860, the villa was an opulent mansion for Philadelphia industrialist, George Allen. After 83 years in the family, the building was sold and sat in disrepair until a couple of vacationers strolled past and wound up buying it in 1994. Renovated completely by the summer of '97, the mansion now has 24 guestrooms to choose from, each of them lavishly and tastefully decorated. Whether you're getting away for the night or for an extended stay, make it a point to wander the award-winning lush gardens on the two-acre property. You may just decide to hold your next big celebration in a tent on the grounds or inside the mansion. During your stay, you'll be treated to genuine southern hospitality, absolute privacy, and gourmet food. *720 Washington Street, 800-381-3888, www.southernmansion.com.*

THE STAR

This is the latest addition to the Congress Hall family – it sits across the street from its big cousin and shares the same bright yellow coloring. The complex consists of four elements – a nine-room Victorian inn, 10 motel units, a pair of two-bedroomed apartments and a coffee shop. The decor throughout is stylish but playful, as witnessed by the leopard-print carpet above. At the inn, most of the rooms have ocean views and all have beautiful ensuite bathrooms. On the first floor is the coffee shop, where guests can enjoy a morning cup on the deck overlooking the ocean. The motel is a smart update of the classic American model – the five first-floor units have private backyard patios, while the second-floor units have decks. Every unit is beautifully furnished and fitted with first-class amenities, including flat-screen TV. The apartments each have two bedrooms and bathrooms and are perfect for large groups or families. *29 Perry Street, (609) 884-4590, www.thestarinn.net.*

THE VIRGINIA HOTEL AND COTTAGE

It's difficult to believe, but Jackson Street used to be something of a forlorn place, and for a while, the Virginia was one of its *least* attractive properties. It's difficult to believe because now Jackson is a glorious street and the Virginia is perhaps its crowning jewel. The hotel was renovated in 1989 with the purpose of providing visitors with the standards expected of a luxury boutique hotel – exquisite taste, fine dining, a relaxed ambience and first-class facilities. It doesn't hurt that the Virginia is a minute's walk from the beach. The hotel has 24 rooms, some of them with private porches, and across the road, at 22 Jackson, there are six suites at the Cottage, an historic property that recently joined the Virginia family. In the hotel's cocktail lounge, guests can sit back and enjoy pianist Steve LaManna or relax on the deck overlooking the street. And the restaurant, The Ebbitt Room, is simply magnificent (see page 126). *25 Jackson Street, (609) 884-5700, www.virginiahotel.com.*

THE THOMAS WEBSTER HOUSE

Proprietors Harry and Berny Gamble resemble a comedy double act. Harry is tall, quiet and dry humored, while Berny is short and bubbly with an engaging sense of humor that makes people feel at home. However, you can tell by the attention to detail in every inch of this wonderful house and its gardens (Harry is a landscape designer) how seriously they take their roles as hosts. The Webster house has four antique-furnished luxury suites, with kitchens, sitting rooms, private baths and best of all, private decks, lovingly landscaped by Harry. Pour yourself a drink, sit back and enjoy this tropical outdoor retreat. *933 Washington St., (609) 898-9248, (856) 459-1008, www.thomaswebsterhouse.com.*

VICTORIAN LACE INN

Like Cape May, the Victorian Lace is a delight all-year-round. In the summer months, you can sip coffee on the front porch as you gaze at the Atlantic, only four doors away, and enjoy its cool breezes, or relax with a drink on a balmy evening. On cooler nights, sit by the crackling fire in the parlor or snuggle up in front of your own private fireplace in one of the inn's gorgeous suites. As if that doesn't sound relaxing enough, the inn's owners also have the Cape May Day Spa (page 177), which means there are great spa packages, including the Romantic Getaway, the Busy Woman's Midweek Getaway, and the Ultimate Spa Package. Children are welcome at the Victorian Lace, which often isn't the case in Cape May. *901 Stockton Ave., (609) 884-1772, www.victorianlaceinn.com.*

CHAPTER SIX
The A-Z

THE A-Z OF CAPE MAY

All addresses are Cape May, unless otherwise stated. The telephone code is 609, unless otherwise stated. NCM denotes North Cape May, while WCM denotes West Cape May. It's possible that some of the numbers may have changed since the book was published. If so, we apologize – we did our best.

AIRPORTS
Atlantic City International (ACY), 645-7895. **Cape May County**, 886-8652 (private aircrafts only). **Philadelphia International (PHL)**, 800-745-4283. **Woodbine**, 861-1300 (private aircraft only).

ARCADES/AMUSEMENTS
Family Fun Arcade, Beach Ave. and Howard. **Victorian Arcade**, 406 Beach Ave. **Morey's Piers**, Schellenger Ave & Boardwalk, Wildwood, 522-3900. **Raging Waters Waterparks**, 25th & Boardwalk & 3501 Boardwalk, 522-5431. **Splash Zone Water Park**, 3500 Boardwalk, Wildwood, 729-5600.

ATMS (SEE ALSO BANKS)
Acme, Lafayette & Ocean. **Atlantic Books**, 500 Washington St. **Carney's**, 411 Beach Avenue. **Collier's Liquor**, 202 Jackson St.; **7-11**, Broadway & Sunset; **Uncle Bill's Pancake House**, Beach & Perry; **Wawa**, Bank and Broad & 1426 Texas Ave.

BABYSITTING
Cape Aware Child Care Inc., 465-0840.

BANKS/CHECK CASHING
Cape Savings, 217 Jackson, 884-0900. **Crest Savings**, 3306 Bayshore Road, NCM, 886-5545. **Fleet**, 315 Ocean St. Unit 3, 884-5500 & 3841 Bayshore Road, NCM, 886-8686. **PNC**, 930 Washington Street, 884-0801 & 3801 Bayshore Road, NCM, 898-2344. **Sturdy Savings**, 701 Washington St, 898-1213 & 3851 Bayshore Rd, 884-5656. **Sun National**, 941 Columbia Av, 898-2120

BASKETBALL COURTS
Wise Anderson Memorial Park, Lafayette St. (next to the Cape May Elementary School)

BATTING CAGES
Lighthouse Putt and Bat, 2576 Rte 9, Ocean View, 624-0719. **Park Place Family Entertainment**, 500 Park Blvd, Wildwood, 522-3300.

THE A-Z OF CAPE MAY

BIKE/SURREY RENTALS
Cape Island, 1111 Beach & 727 Beach 884-8011, www.capeislandbikerentals.com. **Shield's**, 11 Gurney St., 884-BIKE (2453). **Steck's**, Beach & Perry St., 884-1188. **Village Bicycle Shop**, 605 Lafayette St., 884-8500

BIRD WATCHING
Cape May Bird Observatory, 701 East Lake Drive, Cape May Point, 884-2736, www.njaudubon.org. **Cape May Point State Park**, 884-2159. **Nature Center of Cape May**, 1600 Delaware Ave., 884-8848, www.njaudubon.org.

BOAT RENTALS
B & E Marine, 626 W. 26th Avenue, Wildwood, 522-6440. **Dad's Place**, 501 Ocean Drive, Wildwood, 522-3911. **Lakeview Docks**, 7116 Park Blvd & Rambler, Wildwood Crest, 522-0471, www.lakeviewdocks.com. **Mocean Water Sports**, 560 W. Rio Grande Ave, Wildwood, 522-3017. **Pier 47 Marina**, 3001 Wildwood Blvd, Wildwood, 729-4774. **Sterling Harbor Bait & Tackle**, 1020 W. Rio Grande Ave, Wildwood, 729-1425, www.sterlingharbor.com.

BOOKSHOPS
Atlantic Books, 711 Beach Avenue, 898-0357 & Decatur & Washington, 898-9694. **Book Shoppe**, 3845 Bayshore Road, NCM.

BOWLING
3 J's Wildwood Bowl, 3401 New Jersey Avenue at Oak, Wildwood, 729-0111.

CAR RENTALS
Alamo Rent A Car, Wildwood, 463-9600. **Just Four Wheels**, 429 W. Rio Grande Ave, Wildwood, 522-0049. **Sunset Auto Rental**, 884-4969. **Wildwood Rent a Car**, 429 W. Rio Grande Ave., Wildwood, 522-0990.

CAR WASHES
T & A Car Wash Plaza, Hwy 47 & 2nd, Rio Grande, 886-1011. **Towne Texaco**, 3731 Bayshore Rd, NCM, 884-8595

CARRIAGE RIDES
Cape May Carriage Co., 641 Sunset Blvd., 884-4466. www.capemaycarriage.com.

CHURCHES/SYNAGOGUES
Allen A.M.E., 717 Franklin St., 884-2626. **Beth Judah Temple**, Spencer Ave., Wildwood,

522-7541. **Cape May Lutheran**, 506 Pittsburgh Ave., 884-2181. **Cape Island Baptist**, Columbia & Gurney St., 884-3917. **Episcopal Church of the Advent**, Franklin & Washington. **First Assembly of God**, 1068 Seashore Rd., Cold Spring, 884-2424. **First United Methodist**, 635 Washington St., 884-3792. **First Presbyterian Church**, Decatur & Hughes St., 884-3949. **Franklin St. Methodist Church**, Lafayette & Franklin. **Macedonia Baptist Church**, Lafayette & Franklin. **Our Lady Star of the Sea**, 525 Washington St., 884-5311.

CONVENIENCE STORES
Egon's North Cape May Market, 3832 Bayshore Road, NCM, 886-3660. **Wawa**, Bayshore & Townbank Rd, NCM; 1426 Texas Ave; Bank & Broad.

CRIB RENTALS
Wildwood Crib Rental, 4903 Pacific Ave, Wildwood, 522-2724.

DANCING LESSONS
Ballroom Dancing Lessons at Congress Hall with instructor Tom Cupp, 888-944-1816.

DOCTORS
Bayshore Medical Associates, 3826 Bayshore Road, NCM, 886-3636. **Cape Pediatrics Associates**, 3806 Bayshore Road, NCM, 886-7733. **Dr. Andrew F. Drake DO**, 1302 Texas Avenue, 884-2010. **Dr. Maroldo & Dr. Boyle, Family Practice & Emergencies**, 650 Townbank Road, NCM, 898-7447. **Atlantic Cumberland Eye Associates**, 937 Columbia Ave, 884-1313. **Dr. Zaheer A. Farooqui MD**, 3018 Bayshore Road, NCM, 886-5637.

DOLPHIN & WHALE WATCHING
Cape May Whale Watcher, sails from Miss Chris Marina, 2nd Ave & Wilson Drive, 800-786-5445, www.capemaywhalewatcher.com. **Cape May Whale Watch & Research Center**, 1286 Wilson Drive, 888-531-0055, www.capemaywhalewatch.com.

DRY CLEANERS
Cape Laundromat & Dry Cleaners, 3704 Bayshore Road, NCM, 886-8083. **Model Cleaners**, 1430 Texas Avenue & 1802 Bayshore Road, Villas, 884-8446, 886-6143. **Plaza Cleaners,** Bayshore and Breakwater Road, 884-5957. **Young's Cleaners**, 3845 Bayshore Road, 898-9894

EYE DOCTOR
Dr. Arlene Gorny, 937 Columbia Ave., 898-0800. **Dr. Robert K. Petrelli**, 1400 New

Jersey Avenue, North Wildwood, 522-4199

FARM MARKETS

Duckies, 736 Broadway, 989-9191. **LeGates**, Bayshore Road NCM, 886-5513. **Leslie Rae Farms**, Stevens St, WCM, 884-4522. **Roadside Bouquets Flower and Honey Farm**, 898-1711. **West Cape May Sunset Farmers Market,** every Tuesday at 3 pm until sunset, 732 Broadway.

FAX SERVICES

Colliers Liquor Store, Jackson & Lafayette, 884-8488. **MagicBrain CyberCafe,** 31 Perry St. **Leader Printers**, 5914 New Jersey Ave, Wildwood Crest, 729-0161.

FERRY

Cape May Lewes Ferry, 889-7200, www.capemaylewesferry.com.

FESTIVALS

June 12 **Victorian Fair, 10 - 4pm, Emlen Physick Estate, 884-5404. July 31** Country Corn Festival at historic Cold Spring Village, 898-2300. August 10 **CM Women's Club Peach Festival**, Bank St. & Lafayette, 10-5pm. September 4 **West Cape May Tomato Festival**, Borough Hall, 884-8382. August 28-29 **Apple Pie Festival** at Historic Cold Spring Village, 898-2300. September 18 - 23 **Food & Wine Festival**, MAC, 884-5404. October 2 **Oktoberfest**, Jackson Street, 884-2664 or 884-2226. October 8 - 17 **Victorian Week**, MAC, 884-5404. October 9 **Lima Bean Festival**, West Cape May, 884-1005. October 23 **Pumpkin Festival** at Historic Cold Spring Village, 898-2300. November 12 - 14 **Cape May Jazz Festival**, 884-7277. November 18 - 21 **Cape May New Jersey State Film Festival**, 884-6700. July 31 **Country Corn Festival** at Historic Cold Spring Village, 898-2300.

FIRE DEPARTMENT

Non-emergency 884-9512

FISHING

Bob Jackson's Surf Fishing Center, 719 Broadway, WCM, 898-7950. **Cold Spring Bait & Tackle**, 970 Hwy 109, 884-2248. **Fiesta**, sails from South Jersey Marina, US HWY 109, 884-3421. **Gallant Lady Fishing Boat**, 1231 Hwy 9, 884-7754. **Miss Cape May**, sails from South Jersey Marina, 884-3421. **Miss Chris**, 3rd Avenue, 884-3939. **Porgy III Deep Sea Fishing**, HWY 109, 884-1214. **Rainbow Deep Sea Fishing**, 1121 HWY 109, 898-2331. **Sea Hunt,** sails from Miss Chris Marina, 884-0909, www.seahunt-fishing.com. **Sportfishing Unlimited**, 866-567-5400. **South Jersey Fishing Center**, HWY 109, 884-

3800. **Storyteller Sportfishing charters**, 888-982-FISH (3474).

GALLERIES

Artists Outlet, 315 Ocean, 898-2000. **Beach Gallery Fine Art**, 312 Beach Ave, 884-5449. **Bob's Art and Framing Gallery**, 600 Park Blvd, 884-9325. **Cape May Art Gallery**, 323 Washington, 884-4803. **Cape May County Art League**, 600 Park Blvd, 884-8628. **Cape May on Canvas**, 318 Washington, 884-3341. **David Dunleavy Cape May Gallery**, 507 Washington, 884-8388. **McDowell's Gallery**, 526 Washington, 884-0430. **Ocean Street Gallery**, 208 Ocean, 884-0088. **Thomas Kinkade at Cranberry Court**, 421 Washington, 898-4200. **Tides of Time**, 31 Perry St. 884-3306. **Washington Commons Gallery**, 315 Ocean, 884-1880. **Washington Street Gallery**, 312 Washington, 884-1818.

GAS STATIONS/AUTO REPAIR

Cape Harbor Auto Repair, 795 St. Hwy 109, 898-0855. **Cape May Exxon Servicenter**, Rte 9, 884-4777. **Cape May Mobil**, Washington & Yacht Aves, 884-4848. **Cape Port Texaco**, 795 St. Hwy 109, 884-1278. **Cremin's North Cape May Citgo**, Bayshore Rd & Washington Blvd, 886-7493. **Steve's Mobil**, Bayshore Rd. & Lincoln Blvd, NCM, 884-6490. **Towne Texaco**, 3731 Bayshore Rd, NCM, 884-8595

GOLF

Cape May National Golf Club, Exit 4A Garden State Parkway, 884-1563, www.cmngc.com. **Cape May Par 3 & Driving Range**, Fulling Mill Rd., Rio Grande. 889-2600.

GYMS

Cape Fitness Center, 600 Park Blvd, 898-1515. **North Beach Health Club**, 3860 Bayshore Rd, NCM 886-4842. **World Gym**, 3845 Bayshore Rd, NCM, 898-3800.

HAUNTED TOUR

Haunted Cape May Tour, tickets at Boo-Tique Shop, Hotel Macomber, 463-8984.

HOSPITAL

Burdette Tomlin Memorial, exit 10 Garden State Parkway, 463-2000.

INTERNET ACCESS

Magic Brain CyberCafé, 31 Perry St., Carpenter's Square Mall, 884-8188,

THE A-Z OF CAPE MAY

www.magicbraincybercafe.com.

KAYAKING

Aqua Trails, 956 Ocean Drive, 884-5600, www.aquatrails.com. **Kayak Rentals and Sales**, 884-3351, Miss Chris Marina, 3rd & Wilson Dr. **Lakeview Docks**, 7116 Park Blvd & Rambler, Wildwood Crest, 522-0471, www.lakeviewdocks.com. **Miss Chris Marina Kayak Sales and Rentals**, 3rd Ave, & Wilson, 884-3351.

KITES

The Great Atlantic Kite Co., 316 Beach Ave, 884-3444. **1900 Kites and Bikes**, 1900 Boardwalk, North Wildwood, 729-7329.

LIBRARY

Cape May City Library, Ocean & Hughes St., 884-9568. **Cape May County Library**, 30 W. Mechanic St., Cape May Court House, 463-6350.

LIGHTHOUSE

Cape May Lighthouse, Lighthouse Road, Cape May Point, 884-5404.

MARINAS

Bree-Zee-Lee Yacht Basin, Ocean Drive, 884-4849. **Cape May Marine**, 1263 Lafayette, 884-0262. **Harbor View Marina**, 954 Ocean Drive, 884-0808. **Hinch Marina**, 989 Ocean Drive, 884-7289. **Mc Duell Marine**, 956 Ocean, 884-0404. **Mill Creek Marina**, Ocean Drive, 884-4391. **Roseman's Boat Yard & Charter Boats**, Roseman Lane, 884-3370. **Snug Harbor Marina**, 926 Ocean Drive, 884-4217. **South Jersey Marina**, HWY 109, 884-2400. **Utsch's Marina**, 1121 Rte. 109, Schellenger's Landing, 884-2051

MASSAGE

Accent on Beauty, 128 Sunset Blvd, WCM, 884-7040. **Cape May Day Spa**, Congress Hall Hotel, 898-2425 & 607 Jefferson St., 898-1003, www.capemaydayspa.com. The Massage Center, Bolero hotel, 3320 Atlantic Ave., Wildwood, 522-9220. **Serenity Day Spa and Salon**, 3704 Bayshore Road, NCM, 889-6900. **Touch & Go Massage**, 972-6260, www.touchandgomassage.com.

MINIATURE GOLF

Cape May Miniature Golf, 315 Jackson St., 884-2222. **Ocean Putt Golf**, 401 Beach Avenue, 884-7808. **Rainbow Ice Cream Palace**, Bayshore & Townbank, NCM, 886-9891. **The Wave**, Pittsburgh & New Jersey Ave.

THE A-Z OF CAPE MAY

MOVIE THEATERS
Bayshore 8, 3860 Bayshore Road, NCM, 889-8800. **Franks Beach 4**, 711 Beach Avenue, 884-4403.

MUSEUMS
Cape May County Historical Musuem, 504 Rte. 9, Cape May Court House 463-3535. **Cold Spring Village**, 729 Route 9 (Seashore Road), 898-2300. **Emlen Physick Estate**, 1048 Washington Street, 884-5404. **Firemen's Museum**, Washington & Franklin. **George F. Boyer Historical Museum**, The Wildwood Historical Society 3907 Pacific Ave., Wildwood (609) 523-0277. **Greater Cape May Historical Society**, Washington and Franklin St., 884-9100. **Naval Air Station Wildwood Aviation Musuem**, 500 Forrestal Rd., Cape May Airport, Rio Grande, 886-8787. **Wildwood Doo Wop Museum**,3201 Pacific Ave., Wildwood 729-4000.

PARASAIL
Peg Leg Parasail, 898-1600, www.peglegparasail.com. **Atlantic Parasail**, 522-1869, www.altanticparasail.com.

PHARMACIES
Acme, 3845 Bayshore Road, NCM, 884-1761 & **Acme**, Washington Commons, 884-7217. **CVS**, 139 Myrtle Ave, WCM, 884-3313. **Eckerd Drugs**, 3233 Bayshore Road, NCM, 886-4214. **Rite Aid**, 3301 Bayshore Road, NCM, 884-5464.

PLAYGROUNDS/PARKS
Harbor View Park, Harbor Lane. **Wise Anderson Memorial Park**, Lafayette St. **Kiwanis Park**, Madison Avenue. **Nature Center**, 1600 Delaware Ave. **Rotary Park**, Lafayette & Decatur. **State Park**, Cape May Point.

POLICE
(Non-emergency) 884-9500.

POST OFFICE
Washington & Franklin St., 884-3578

RECYCLING
Cape May City, 884-9591
Cape May County Recycles, 465-9026

THE A–Z OF CAPE MAY

REALTORS

By the Sea Realty, 411-413 Park Blvd, 884-3050. **Cape May Realty**, 311 Pittsburgh Ave., 884-2700. **Century 21 – Cape Shore Realty**, 3844 Bayshore Road, NCM, 886-7777. **Century 21 – Gilmartin & Co.**, 1382 Lafayette, 884-1800. **Century 21 Premier Realty**, 889-1700. **Chris Clemans & Co.**, 1159 Washington St. at Union, 884-3332, www.chrisclemans.com. **Coastline Realty**, 1400 Texas Avenue, 884-5005, www.coastlinerealty.com. **Coldwell Banker James C. Otton Real Estate**, 3840 Bayshore Road, NCM, 886-8101. **Coldwell Banker Sol Needles**, 512 Washington Mall, 884-8428, www.coldwellbankercapemay.com. **Dellas Agency**, 309 Decatur, 884-3488, www.dellasagency.com. **Hanscomb Realty**, 917 Madison Ave, 884-3330. **Farrell Realty**, 3821 Bayshore Road, NCM, 886-0010. **Fleming Real Estate**, 1484 Washington, 884-0033. **Homestead Real Estate Co.**, 846 Broadway, WCM, 884-1888. **Jersey Cape Realty**, 739 Washington, 884-5800. **Manzoni Realty**, 937 Columbia, 898-8200 & 3315 Bayshore Rd., NCM, 884-2323, www.manzonirealty.com. **Roth's Real Estate**, 600 Park Blvd, WCM, 884-2806. **Schick Realty**, 3842 Bayshore Rd, NCM, 886-1101. **Tolz Realtors**, Lafayette & Madison, 884-7001.

RESTROOMS

Ocean St. at Washington Commons; Decatur St. (between Mall & Lyle Lane); Transportation Center (Lafayette & Elmira); Beach & Broadway; Promenade at Beach near Grant St.; Convention Hall; Beach & Philadelphia Ave.; New Jersey Ave. & Wilmington Ave.; Trenton & Beach Ave.

SALONS

Cape May Day Spa, Congress Hall Hotel, 898-2425 & 607 Jefferson St., 898-1003, www.capemaydayspa.com. **Hairloom in Sunbow**, 1061 Seashore Road, 884-7139. **John's Barber and Style Shop**, 1352 Washington Avenue, 884-1274. **TJ Barber shop**, 3802 Bayshore Road, NCM, 886-0122. **Accent on Beauty**, 128 Sunset Blvd, WCM, 884-7040. **Amy's La Casa Bella**, 522 Shunpike, 884-4815. **Artizan Salon and Spa**, 600 Park Blvd., WCM, 884-4499. **Global Wave Inc.**, 620 Hughes, 884-0251. **Hair Cuttery**, Bayshore Mall, NCM, 884-5854. **The Hair Station**, 3856 Bayshore Road, NCM, 886-7600. **Head to Toe**, 848 Broadway, WCM, 898-9646. **Lorraine's Hair Salon at the Grand Hotel**, Beach Ave., 898-0622. **Serenity Day Spa and Salon**, 3704 Bayshore Road, NCM, 889-6900. **Shear Sunsations**, 1400 Texas Avenue, 884-3011. **Teaser's**, 2505 Bayshore Road, NCM, 889-9344. **Today's Hair**, Breakwater Plaza, NCM, 898-8399.

SHUTTLE BUS

Cape Area Transit (CAT). Route begins at the Transportation Center, travels down

Lafayette to Cape May Elementary. Stops include Lobster House, Physick Estate & Utsch's Marina.

SURFING LESSONS
Ocean Outfitters, Wildwood Crest, 729-7400.

SWIMMING POOLS
Joseph Von Savage Memorial Pool, 8800 New Jersey Avenue, Wildwood, 522-0084. **Cape May Recreation**, 884-9565.

TAILORS
Young's Cleaners, 3845 Bayshore Road, NCM, 898-9894. **Model Cleaners**, 1430 Texas Avenue, 884-8446. **Plaza Cleaners,** Bayshore and Breakwater Road, 884-5957

TAXICABS
AAA Cape Cab Co., 884-2273. **Aarts Cape May Taxi,** 898-RIDE. **Victorian Cape Limousine**, 886-0111. **Villas Taxis**, 889-8799.

TEA ROOM
Twinings Tearoom at the Emlen Physick Estate, 1048 Washington Street, 884-5404, www.capemaymac.org

TENNIS COURTS
William J. Moore Tennis Club, 1020 Washington Street. 884-8986. **Wise Anderson Memorial Park**, Lafayette St.

THEATER
Cape May Stage, professional equity theatre, 884-1341, www.capemaystage.com. **East Lynne Theater Company**, 121 Fourth Ave.,WCM, 884-5898, www.eastlynnecompany.org . **Elaine's Dinner Theater**, 513 Lafayette Street, www.elainesdinnertheater.com, 884-4358.

TRAIN
Cape May Seashore Lines, 884-2675

TRANSPORTATION
New Jersey Transit, 800-772-3606. **Transportation Center,** Lafayette & Ocean, 884-9562.

THE A-Z OF CAPE MAY

TROLLEY TOURS
Mid-Atlantic Center for the Arts guided tours, 884-5404.

UMBRELLA RENTALS
Steger Beach Service, 884-3058

VINEYARD
Cape May Winery & Vineyard, 709 Townbank Road, NCM, 884-1169.
Turdo Vineyards, 3911 Bayshore Road, NCM, 898-3424.

VETERINARIANS
Cape May Veterinary Hospital, 694 Petticoat Creek Lane, NCM, 884-1729.

VIDEO STORES
Bayshore Mall Video, 3845 Bayshore Road, NCM, 884-0400. Blockbuster Video, 1432 Texas Ave, 884-7741. **Perry Street Video**, 484 Perry St., WCM, 884-8742.

WAVERUNNERS
Crest Watersports, 6200 Park Blvd. & Sweetbriar Rd, at the Starlight Fleet, Wildwood Crest, 522-5926. **Lakeview Docks**, 7116 Park Blvd & Rambler, Wildwood Crest, 522-0471. **Mocean Water Sports**, 560 W. Rio Grande Ave, Wildwood, 522-3017.

WEDDINGS
Weddings By the Sea, 139 N. Broadway, 884-7900, www.weddings-bythesea.com.
Vital Statistics Office, 884-9599.

WELCOME CENTERS
Cape May Chamber of Commerce Welcome Center, located at the transportation center, Lafayette & Ocean, 884-5508.. **Washington Street Mall Information Booth**, Washington St. Mall at Ocean.

YOGA
Cape May Yoga, Washington Commons, 315 Ocean St., 884-3200. **Yoga on the Lawn**, Congress Hall hotel, 884-8421, www.congresshall.com. **Yoga By the Sea**, 898-0383.

ZOO
Cape May County Park & Zoo, Exit 11 Garden State Parkway, 465-5271, www.capemaycountyzoo.com.

Acknowledgements

DON POCHER For lending the beautiful old postcards that were used as opening chapter illustrations.

DAVE RODRIGUES Of MagicBrain Computing for preventing this book from falling into a technological black hole.

ANNIE MULLOCK For offering a constant stream of support, interesting salads and comfort food.

MIKE DEMUSZ For beautifully illustrating the covers in about the time it takes to boil an egg.

MARK CHAMBERLAIN For paying in advance.

BARRY RONK For the camera.

PAUL JACOBSEN Of ASAP Printing for being the man with the scans at just the right time – again.

ZOEY SLESS-KITAIN & STEPHEN SPAGNUOLA For the lovely photographs, at such short notice.

TRACEY MARTIN Whose brillyant proofreeding maid sure there wasn't wun singel typo in this vook.

Further Reading

That's easy! Just make sure you read *Exit Zero*, the periodical that comes out every week in summer and, well, periodically in spring, winter and fall. To subscribe, visit us at www.exitzero.us

Beach Plum Press